BAGGAGE CLAIM

Renewing Your Mind for Marriage

BAGGAGE CLAIM

Renewing Your Mind for Marriage

Pastor Willie Marshall

Unless otherwise indicated, all Scripture quotations are taken from The King James Version of the Bible. Scripture quotations are from THE AMPLIFIED BIBLE, Copyright © 1954, 1958, 1962, 1964, 1965, 1987 by The Lockman Foundation. All rights reserved. Used by permission. (www.Lockman. "Scripture quotations are taken from the Amplified® Bible (AMP), Copyright © 2015 by The Lockman Foundation. Used by permission. www.Lockman.org" "Scripture taken from the New Century Version. Copyright © 1987, 1988, 1991 by Thomas Nelson, Inc. Used by permission. All rights reserved." Scripture quotations are taken from the Holy Bible, New Living Translation, copyright ©1996, 2004, 2007, 2013, 2015 by Tyndale House Foundation. Used by permission of Tyndale House Publishers, Inc., Carol Stream, Illinois 60188. All rights reserved. "Scripture is taken from The Message. Copyright © 1993, 1994, 1995, 1996, 2000, 2001, 2002. Used by permission of NavPress Publishing Group." The Message is quoted: "Scripture taken from The Message. Copyright © 1993, 1994, 1995, 1996, 2000, 2001, 2002. Used by permission of NavPress Publishing Group."

BAGGAGE CLAIM
Renewing Your Mind for Marriage

Copyright © 2023
ISBN: 978-1-7360064-6-7
Published by R.M.P.

Subjects: Marriage | Empowerment | Growth

All rights reserved under International Copyright Law. Contents and/or cover may not be reproduced in whole or in part, in any form, or by any means, without the express written consent of the author.

Printed in the United States of America

Dedication

This book is dedicated to the loving memories of my mother, Betty Jean Marshall, and my grandmother, WillieMae Marshall, who showed me how to trust God and talk to Him. It's because of their prayers and their sacrifices that I am who I am today. I'm forever grateful for them.

I also dedicate this book to my beautiful wife, Sophina, who has had my back since day one. She has stood with me, believed in me, prayed for me, and encouraged me. Together, we have learned to trust God and watch Him work. She is a devoted wife, my best friend, and a loving mother to my son, my partner, and my confidante. I thank God for her often for her commitment to the vision and her willingness to stand beside me, living an exceptional life of faith.

To our son Prince, who has been a faithful non-complaining son. Thank you for your timely reminders of what you've heard daddy preach. You are an amazing son, and you often inspire me to keep going. Thank you for believing in daddy. Your mother and I are very proud of you.

Finally, this book is dedicated to couples who are serious about their marriage relationship. To couples who are ready to get married but want to learn how to do marriage God's way. It is my heart's desire that you will receive and apply the principles in this book to cause success in your marriage. Remember, marriage is God's idea, and you can have a prevailing marriage if you choose to do marriage God's way. If you embody the information and revelation that you will receive from the pages of this book, you will improve the quality of your marriage and life.

Table of Contents

Appreciation 9

Introduction 11

Chapter 1. His and Her Baggage 13

Chapter 2. What's In Your Baggage? 25

Chapter 3. Who Packed Your Baggage? 39

Chapter 4. Unpacking the Baggage 55

Chapter 5. New Mind 77

Chapter 6. Breaking the Habits of
                  Bad Baggage Packing 93

Chapter 7. Guard Your Heart Protect Your Mind 107

Chapter 8. A New Mind Repacked 113

Bio 125

Appendix

Appreciation

Our special thanks go to the following people:

To our spiritual parents in the faith, Apostle I.V. Hilliard and Pastor Bridget Hilliard. Thank you for your demonstration of faith and your example of what marriage should be and look like. The Bible tells us to follow those who, through faith and patience, inherited the promise. And the life you both live has been on display for us and countless others to follow. Thank you for teaching us how to trust God, have faith in God, and believe in God. It is because of your teachings of God's Word and demonstrations of faith do we stand strong in faith today. We thank you.

To Pastor Debbie Comellas, Pastor Vana Payne, and the NTWC family. We are so greatly appreciative of your prayers, your belief in us, and your financial support. During some of the most challenging faith moments of our ministry, you'll have partnered with us. Thank you for the encouraging words of faith and motivation to keep pressing. We thank you so much for reminding us that we are not by ourselves. We thank you.

To my dear brother and friend, Dr. Vincent Robinson, Lead Pastor of Right way Christian Center. Bro, I'm so grateful and appreciative of you as a friend. You have motivated me by your words of faith and inspired me by your actions of faith. I'm thankful to God for the divine connection. It's because of you sharing your wisdom and insight on scribing that the Lord reignited my heart to get in pursuit of my passion for writing. I'm blessed to have you as an AIM brother in Christ. We thank you.

To my big brother in the faith, Pastor Patrick Ligon Sr., pastor of Great Faith Church. Thank you for your timely and inspiring words of faith. I'm so appreciative of your wisdom nuggets during our times of conversation. Thank you for opening up your behind-the-scenes and showing me another way of enhancing ministry. We are thankful for you and Angela's display of being one and enjoying ministry and marriage. We thank you.

Introduction

BAGGAGE CLAIM

It is my prayer and belief that this book will take your marriage to the next level. I believe that this book will be a game changer for you and your marriage. Everybody would love to have a game-changer on their team like Kobe Bryant, LeBron James, or Michael Jordan. Why would you want them on your team? Other people on the team were good, but these specific individuals were game-changers. These were the people who had what it took to get you to the finish line, the ones to shoot that game-changing three Pointer. These were the individuals you wanted to put the ball in the hand of when the game was on the line. This book will be a game changer for you and your marriage.

In this book, I want to expose you to what's making the decisions in your life, and it's probably not what you think it is. You will learn that you're not the one making the decisions like you think you are. So then, what's making the decision to behave the way that you are? Is it you? What's making the decision to think the way that you do? Is it you? What is making the decision to respond the way that you do? Is it you?

Introduction

What's making the decision to talk to your spouse the way that you do? Is it you? What's making the decision for you to spend or manage your money the way that you do? Is it you? Now, this book is not just for the relationship of marriage but any relationship you may be in, including your relationship with Christ.

When you get to the end of this book, you will discover what's been controlling your decision-making and how to change it. This change will be the game changer needed for your marriage to prevail.

For clarity, when I say baggage, it is a metaphor for the mind. When I say claim, it is your acceptance of what's been packed in your baggage, your mind.

Chapter 1

His and Her Baggage

Then the LORD God made a woman from the rib he had taken out of the man, and he brought her to the man. The man said, "This is now bone of my bones and flesh of my flesh; she shall be called 'woman,' for she was taken out of man." That is why a man leaves his father and mother and is united to his wife, and they become one flesh.

> *Then the Lord God made a woman from the rib he had taken out of the man, and he brought her to the man. ²³ The man said, "This is now bone of my bones and flesh of my flesh; she shall be called 'woman, for she was taken out of man." ²⁴ That is why a man leaves his father and mother and is united to his wife, and they become one flesh.*
> **Genesis 2:22-24 NIV**

Becoming One

In these verses, we see the story of Eve being brought to Adam for the very first time, and in verse 24, it reads, and they become one flesh. The becoming one is the process of learning each other. When you first met your spouse, you came with your baggage already packed. Why is it a process of learning each other? Because when y'all came together, y'all both came from different backgrounds, different life experiences, different views, different past relationships, different upbringings, different tastes, different traditions, different styles, different personalities, different income, having different credit, different spending habits, different political views, different skill sets. This is why it is a process to become one because you both come into the relationship with all types of differences.

Now, when you become one, you should think of your marriage as a team of two amazing, unique individuals. The team is what makes it one, but there are two individuals on the team. So that means that you and your spouse have differences. You're not trying to change each other but respect each other's differences and make them work. Because there are some differences that you may have that don't work for your marriage, you need to be responsible and change them. Becoming one means you get to play, work, and grow together. In order to successfully become one, you must change your mindset and see marriage as a team. Becoming one means you get to make decisions together. Your opinion matters because the choices that you make impact your marriage and your spouse. Becoming one means you resolve your marriage issues together. Issues like sex, life, children's activities, money, etc., you get to resolve together and not always run to your parents. When you resolve your issues together, it helps with communication and a better understanding of each other.

My wife and I call our marriage team Marshall. Because we see our marriage as a team, and we work together to protect our team, to strengthen our team, to build our team, to invest in our team, and the list goes on. We have an affirmation that we confess that says: together forever, our marriage is tougher than leather. That's what we confess because we are team Marshall. So, when the water starts to boil in our marriage, we take the pot off the stove. That means we take a break and then reconvene at a later time. At least one of us has to remember that we are team Marshall, so we have to resolve this thing. We are tougher than leather, so we will get through this. The only thing that can tear the toughness of our leather is us from the inside. This is why you must learn to become one; it will strengthen your marriage.

What Makes Becoming One So Difficult?

I'm sure by now you can start to see the need for becoming a team. But what happens when you see yourself as a team but don't function as a team? When you know to make decisions together, but you don't, and you think your decision is the only one and the right one for you to go with. As a team, you're not resolving your problems together, although you know you should. Or you'd rather get counsel from the ungodly outside of your marriage who'd rather have you do things their way and not God's way. So, what makes becoming one so difficult to do? It is because becoming one is something that takes effort and persistence. This will not take place instantly, but with wisdom and effort, it can and will happen. You must be willing to put in the work; if you put in the required work, the marriage will work. When you don't, it doesn't work.

For a dream comes with much business and painful effort, and a fool's voice with many words.
Ecclesiastes 5:3 AMPC

Now, Baggage Claim is not just for your marriage relationship with your spouse but also your marriage relationship with Jesus. Because you can take your baggage into your relationship with Jesus. Some of your marriage issues are happening because your relationship with Jesus is not where it needs to be. If the relationship with Jesus is where it should be, your spouse should be receiving the overflow of that relationship into them.

The Merger

Another way of looking at becoming one is like having a merger. Companies do this all the time: two separate entities combine forces and become one. Exxon and Mobil, America Online (AOL) and Time Warner, H. J. Heinz, and Kraft Foods. These companies all had mergers; they joined forces and became one. And so, it is in marriage two different people, two different races, two different backgrounds, etc., and their becoming one. The key here is two different individuals becoming one. It's not a merger if the same company joins itself. And it's in the becoming one where the issues begin to surface. To better understand the two shall become one flesh or the marriage merger, we need to take a look at the Law of Possession.

The Law of Possession

That is why a man leaves his father and mother and is united to his wife, and they become one flesh.
Genesis 2:24 NIV

To understand the law of possession, you must first understand that God designed married couples to be one. One emotionally, one spiritually, one mentally, one physically, one financially. Although my wife has her own personal checking account, my name is still on the account because we are one. I have my own personal checking account, but my wife's name is on that account as well because we are one. Some may say that I need my own account and my spouse does not need to be on there. Now granted, if your spouse has a spending money problem or gambling issue, and for the financial security of the family, you keep them separate from that checking account, that's another type of situation. But beyond those special types of situations, some may still say that they do not want their spouse on their account for all kinds of reasons. I would have to ask, why do you feel that way? Or think that way? Something has been packed into your baggage that causes you to think the way that you do. And you brought that type of baggage into your current marriage relationship. And this type of baggage can cause unnecessary problems in your marriage. The Law of Possession is simply that you have to share everything in marriage. Anything you don't share can destroy the marriage.

The Marriage Relationship Parallels Our Relationship with Jesus

So likewise, whoever of you does not forsake all that he has cannot be My disciple.
Luke 14:33 NKJV

Also read Ephesians 5

Anything we would not give up for Jesus is an idol and will prevent an intimate relationship between us. For intimacy to occur, there must be total surrender. For oneness to occur, complete surrender must take place. Things that were individually owned and administered before marriage must now become co-owned and co-administered. The only way two things can become one is for there to be a total merger of both parts into one. My wife has access to my cell phone lock code, my email addresses, my bank accounts, which are our bank accounts, all social media accounts, etc. And I have access to all of hers because we are one. The very next day after we got married, we immediately went and changed her last name on all her identifications; we placed our names on each other's bank accounts because there was a merger that had taken place. We became the Marshalls. We keep things transparent, and we share things together because it's a law. When a law is violated, there are consequences. When the law of gravity is violated foolishly, a price is paid.

Why Is This So Difficult For Us To Do?

Why is it so difficult to obey the law of possession? Although we see what the Word of God says, why is it so difficult to respect, obey, and do what is written in God's Word for me to do? Why do I reject God's Word? What is it that's causing this Law of Possession not to be fulfilled? Just Like in your new life with Christ, when you became saved, the only thing that took place is that you became spiritually alive. Your Soulish man was still the same. What's your Soulish man? You're mind, your will, your imagination, your intellect, and your emotion which composes your thinking. That part of you did not change just because you gave your life to Christ. And that did not change; just because you got married to your spouse, your thinking remained the same. Your thinking is still the same because your mind has not yet been renewed. When you look in the Bible, Romans, chapter 10 reveals to us how to give our life to Christ. After you have given your life to Christ comes Romans chapter 12. This chapter reveals to us now that you have given your life to Christ, you need to become transformed by the renewing of your mind. So, just like your marriage to Jesus Christ when you got saved, your mind had not been renewed, so it is when you are married to your spouse, your mind is still the same. The becoming one is a process. You have to learn how to become one and how to become that team of two. You came into your marriage with a lot of differences in the way you were taught about relationships, which could've been in error, a bad relationship that you had, things that you were taught by visualization, things that were poured into you from siblings; all these differences shaped the way you think. These are things that were packed into your baggage that you brought into your relationship with your spouse. That baggage is your mind, and that mind is what you brought into your relationship with Christ and your relationship with your spouse. To take it even a step further, you brought that baggage into relationships you had prior to you getting married. Because of this, it can affect other relationships, your relationships with your siblings, your relationships with your children, and your relationships with friends. Have you ever noticed how nasty your attitude can be at times? Why do you act this way? Have you ever noticed when you're mad because of selfish reasons, you don't want your spouse to touch you? Why do you act this way? Have you noticed the way that you talk to your spouse when you don't get your way? Why do you act this way? What's causing you to make the decision to behave that way and talk sarcastic and in a disrespectful way to your spouse? So why is it so difficult to become one, you ask? It's because something has been packed into our minds where we know better, but we don't do better because you're not the one making the decisions. Now, you may think that it's you, but keep reading, and we will discover the truth of what's making the decisions. I'm not saying you're possessed, but there's something making decisions in your life, and you think it's you, but is it?

We are Selfish Beings

When we come into relationships, we come in as selfish beings. We are very selfish; we want what we want or else. I want mine; I want it this way, and I won't have it any other way. Selfishness is one of the major enemies of married life and love within the family. It affects how we talk to each other, how we divide responsibilities in the home, how we resolve conflicts, and even how we spend our time. It prevents a couple from growing together in marriage.

The goal is to learn how to be selfless, not selfish. Marriage is about servanthood, two selfless individuals who are willing to serve each other. But when you are selfish, you make it all about you. When you're selfish, you don't want to meet your spouse's needs because you make what they need about you. In other words, if it's not convenient for you, then you don't want to meet their needs. Or you say things like you don't need sex right now, you don't need security right now, you don't need leadership right now, you don't need open, honest communication right now, you don't need to be respected right now. And this selfishness is displayed by your attitude, by your actions, by your demeanor, and by your words. Have you ever fixed your spouse a plate of food and served it with an attitude because you didn't feel like serving? Have you ever, during sex, intentionally laid there like a log and not participated because you did not want to minister to your spouse's needs? Are you selfish, or are you serving? Well, those types of actions are called selfishness because you made what they needed about you and not about meeting their need.

Have you ever been to an upscale restaurant? Your expectations were high because this restaurant came highly recommended, but after being seated at the table, you noticed your server had an attitude, rarely came around, spilled your drink while pouring it several different times, and just provided terrible service. How would that make you feel? I know I would ask for their manager and want that server replaced immediately, and that will probably be my last time attending that restaurant. Well, if you don't like that type of service, why would you want to extend that type of service to your spouse? Where you always have an excuse for your poor service and poor attitude with your poor service. Plainly put, that's selfish.

Each spouse's selfishness tends to be the biggest problem in marriage. Those desires that battle within you are selfish desires. This is where the fighting and quarreling come from.

For all that is in the world—the lust of the flesh, the lust of the eyes, and the pride of life—is not of the Father
but is of the world
I John 2:16 NKJV

What causes fights and quarrels among you? Don t they come from your desires that battle within you?
James 4:1 NIV

God Wants Us in Unity

Behold, how good and how pleasant it is For brethren to dwell together in unity!
Psalm 133:1 KJV

And the LORD said, Behold, the people is one, and they have all one language; and this they begin to do: and now nothing will be restrained from them, which they have imagined to do - Genesis 11:6 KJV. So, we see here in Psalms 133:1 that God wants us to be in unity. When we are operating in unity as one like a team, more can be accomplished. Even when the Tower of Babel was being constructed, they operated in the principle of unity. The Bible records in Genesis 11:6, "and now nothing will be restrained from them which they have imagined to do." Why? Because they were in unity, operating as a team, moving as one. Now, these groups of people that were building the tower were not building the tower to glorify God; they wanted to make a name for themselves. In other words, God did not tell them to build this tower, yet they were progressing along to accomplish their goals by applying the principle of unity. If you work at the principle of unity, becoming one with your spouse, nothing will be restrained that you'll imagine to do.

Please understand the devil doesn't want us together operating as one. And he will do all he can to keep you at odds with each other. Chaos and turmoil are what the devil wants for your marriage.

The Bible tells us in First Corinthians 14:33, "For God is not the author of confusion, but of peace, as in all churches of the saints." Satan wants to wreak havoc in your marriage and destroy your union. He doesn't want you to have peace because of unity.

Allow Me to Introduce You to Diablos – The Accuser of the Brethren

And I heard a loud voice saying in heaven, Now is come salvation, and strength, and the kingdom of our God, and the power of his Christ: for the accuser of our brethren is cast down, which accused them before our God day and night.
Revelation 12:10

According to Sermonindex.net, Diablos means a false accuser, slanderer (one who utters false charges or misrepresentations which defame and damage another's reputation), backbiting (malicious comment about one not present), one given to malicious gossip or a calumniator (one who utters maliciously false statements, charges, or imputations about, this term imputes malice to the speaker and falsity to the assertions). Diablos, as a noun, not only describes those who bring false charges against one but also those who disseminate the truth concerning a man and do so maliciously, insidiously, and with hostility.

The accuser, Satan (Diablos), continues to point out flows and magnifies shortcomings and constantly reminds us of what our spouse did to us, our friends, our parents, our siblings, and our neighbors did to us that we did not like. Five ways Diablos accuses: Me to God, God to me, me to my spouse, my spouse to me, me to myself.

Me to God: God, look at them; they're doing it again, the same sin. God to me: see, God didn't come through for you. He said He would, and you still don't have it. Me to my spouse: see, he said he wasn't going to do it again. He still hasn't changed. He's the same person he used to be. My spouse to me: she's still lying. She continues to lie. She's doing the same thing again she said she would never do. Me to myself: you can't do it; you thought you could, you said you would, but you still haven't done it. You are a failure, you are a loser, you are a quitter.

Diablos wants us to hang on to past hurts to keep us at odds with each other so we can't move forward. He consistently reminds us of what has been done to us by loved ones. But God wants us to forgive so we can move forward with peace.

And their sins and iniquities will I remember no more.
Hebrews 10:17

God forgives and forgets, so every time someone wants to remind us of what we did to bring shame and guilt is of the devil. So don't allow him Diablos to use you to tear down your own marriage through accusations. You must forgive; God wants you to, and God tells you to.

> *And when ye stand praying, forgive, if ye have ought against any: that your Father also which is in heaven may forgive you your trespasses. ²⁶But if ye do not forgive, neither will your Father which is in heaven forgive your trespasses.*
> **Mark 11:25-26**

Forgiveness doesn't make them right; it just makes us free. Unforgiveness is like an invisible umbilical cord that keeps us connected to and emotionally feeding from the negative people, places, and experiences of our past. We must pull down the thoughts that the enemy uses to remind us of our spouses' shortcomings. The Apostle Paul wrote this as it concerns the past.

> *Brethren, I count not myself to have apprehended: but this one thing I do, forgetting those things which are behind, and reaching forth unto those things which are before, ¹⁴I press toward the mark for the prize of the high calling of God in Christ Jesus.*
> **Philippians 3:13–14**

Although we are not God to forget, we can pull the negative memories of the past that Diablos uses as accusations. We must intentionally pull down the negative thoughts that the enemy places in our minds. When we pull them down, we are no longer looking back but pressing forward to becoming one.

Chapter 2

What's In Your Baggage?

There is a common statement I've heard from many married couples that I've had the privilege of counseling. And that statement is, " I didn't sign up for this." The reason they say this is because they are now dealing with the baggage of their spouse, and it feels overbearing to them. And my response is always yes, you did sign up for this. It is in the vow that you made before saying I do. Traditional vows are generally made in this manner. "In the name of God, I, ____, take you, ____, to be my wife/husband, to have and to hold from this day forward, for better, for worse, for richer, for poorer, in sickness and in health, forsaking all others, until parted by death. This is my solemn vow." Now, these are the vows of commitment that you made or similar. So when everything is going great, and the money is rolling in, everybody is happy. But when your spouse loses their job, and bills are coming in more than the money, so you can't shop like you used to or travel like you used to, here comes the attitude. You made a vow that said for richer or for poorer. What about in sickness and in health? There are spouses who bail out of their marriage when their spouse becomes seriously ill or even bedridden. But the vow that sums it up is for better or for worse. It's easy to stick together when things are going well. But what makes a person walk out when things are worse? What's making the decision in you to leave when things are not better? Now, in this chapter, we want to take a look at what's packed in your baggage, not your spouse's. So that you understand, you did sign up for better, for worse, for richer, for poorer, in sickness and in health, forsaking all others until parted by death. You signed up for all of that when you got married.

Vows

Vows involve greater accountability and solemnity than do promises. You may promise to take your spouse on vacation, but because of certain circumstances that arise, you may have to break that promise. On the other hand, if you vow before others that you will love and honor your spouse all the days of your life, circumstances should not cause you to break this vow. I am also held to greater accountability by God because your vow was also to God. Let's look at the following scripture.

When thou vowest a vow unto God, defer not to pay it; for he hath no pleasure in fools: pay that which thou hast vowed. ⁵Better is it that thou shouldest not vow, than that thou shouldest vow and not pay. ⁶Suffer not thy mouth to cause thy flesh to sin; neither say thou before the angel, that it was an error: wherefore should God be angry at thy voice, and destroy the work of thine hands? ⁷For in the multitude of dreams and many words there are also divers vanities: but fear thou God.
Ecclesiastes 5:4-7KJV

In the New International Version, it reads,

When you make a vow to God, do not delay to fulfill it. He has no pleasure in fools; fulfill your vow. ⁵It is better not to make a vow than to make one and not fulfill it. ⁶Do not let your mouth lead you into sin. And do not protest to the temple messenger, "My vow was a mistake." Why should God be angry at what you say and destroy the work of your hands? ⁷Much dreaming and many words are meaningless. Therefore fear God.
Ecclesiastes 5:4-7NIV

When you get married, you're getting married in holy matrimony. What makes it holy is because It's sacred. You are dedicating your marriage to God to do marriage His way. When you say your vows, you are not only saying them to each other but also to God. God takes vows seriously. A vow to God is a solemn promise made before God or to God. It is an earnest promise or pledge or personal commitment to perform a specified act or behave in a certain manner, especially a solemn promise to live and act in accordance with the rules. It is the ultimate commitment to God. It is to make a determined decision or promise to do something. A vow is an oath, and God expects us to fulfill any vow made to him.

If a man vow a vow unto the LORD, or swear an oath to bind his soul with a bond; he shall not break his word, he shall do according to all that proceeded out of his mouth.
Numbers 30:2 KJV

"Again, you have heard that it was said to the people long ago, 'Do not break your oath, but fulfill to the Lord the vows you have made.... 'All you need to say is simply 'Yes' or 'No'; anything beyond this comes from the evil one.
Matthew 5:33,37 NIV

To fulfill is to bring to realization. That is, that which you have promised, you make to happen. You are admonished to be a man or woman of integrity. God does not forget vows made to him; watch what comes out of your mouth. It is better not to vow anything than to vow and not fulfill it. Breaking a vow made to God is a sin, and it has consequences. So, never make a hasty vow. A vow to God is extremely binding, and you have to keep it. However, a broken vow should be taken to God in true confession so that God can forgive. Your integrity is at stake when making vows, so before making any at all, you must understand what it is and what it involves. Never rush to make a vow. Be a man or woman of integrity.

Yes, You did Sign Up for This.

So, we can now see, based on the vows we made, that we did indeed sign up for this. You are supposed to do your part in the marriage relationship, keeping your vows of commitment. How do you keep your vows of Commitment? Love. Love is not a chemical but a decision you make. It has nothing to do with your feelings. You decide if you choose to love your spouse. I tell my wife that I love her, so I'm saying that I'm committed to meeting her needs. No other females' needs are met this way. You may see other attractive individuals of the opposite sex, but because of my commitment and my vows to " forsake all others," loving my wife, the other don't matter.

Since you are now married and living with your spouse, learning about them and seeing what they are all about, you are starting to rethink things because you didn't know certain things about them. The way they talk to you when they're angry, their attitude when they don't get their way, they have good priorities but out of order, sex which used to be all the time is now once every blue moon, no more gift giving although the money is there for it, and the list goes on. Here comes the thought: I didn't sign up for this. Yes, you did. Your spouse came into the relationship with baggage, just like you. But because you are so focused on their baggage, you can't see what is stored in yours.

Having False Expectations

A lot of couples, when they come into a marriage, have these false expectations of what a husband is supposed to do and what a wife is supposed to do. Here are some false expectations:

Wife's false expectations

- He is supposed to always take care of me by paying all my bills. And buying me what I want all the time. And he has me, so that should be good enough for him.
- I don't have to help him that's his responsibility.
- He should take care of my kids and me before his kids that don't even live with us.
- He is supposed to be a man and put up with me talking to him like a child.
- That's my daddy; he comes before my husband.
- My money is my money, and your money is my money.

Husband's false expectations

- She is supposed to do all the cooking and cleaning and take care of the children. Then meet my sexual needs with joy and enthusiasm.
- She should do what I say and ask no questions.
- That's my Momma; she comes before my Wife.
- I can have female friends, but you can't have male friends.
- She does as I say; I am her head.

The question is, where did this thinking come from? Who put this in your baggage? Who said that your spouse is supposed to be that way? Who told you that marriage should be like that? God created marriage, not your parents. Now, this is not a knock-on parents because I have parents, and I am a parent. But if what I received from them by example or by conversation doesn't line up with God's word on marriage, I have to reject that teaching. A lot of issues happen in marriages when spouses run back to their parents, sharing the dirty laundry about their spouse with their parents. As a result, your parents now have an issue with your spouse. All this because you painted the negative picture regarding your spouse's baggage but covered yours.

Many people come into marriage with preconceived notions as to what marriage is supposed to be like. And you say I'm going to marry you, but if you ever change, I'm going to unmarry you. Now, you can still be married to them legally, but you unmarried them in your commitment to love them. The baggage that most couples bring into marriage has been packed with conditional love. You say, if these conditions are met, I will love you; if these conditions are not met, I will not love you. Although you chose to stay, you also chose not to meet their greatest needs. Your mind and your money are somewhere else. The wife dresses up, looks beautiful, and smells amazing all when going to work, but never for her husband at home. The husband hangs out with the fellas and spends money but doesn't spend any money and time at home with his wife and kids. The love that should be displayed is unconditional love, where you say the reason. I love you because I choose to love you, not because of what you do for me or to me. So, even when I'm angry at you, I choose to love you. Even when I don't like you at the moment, I choose to love you. Even when you forgot to pay the bill, and the lights went off, I still choose to love you. I choose to love you; I choose to uphold and honor my vow. This is Agape, unconditional love.

But God demonstrates his own love for us in this: While we were still sinners, Christ died for us.
Romans 5:8 NIV

Where Did You Get That From? God Created Marriage

I have to inform you that your daddy, your momma, or your kin folk did not create marriage. Nor did your favorite love novel. Not even your favorite star on your favorite soap opera, etc. So, where did you get these preconceived notions from?

Preconceived means an idea, or opinion formed before having the evidence of its truth are usefulness.

Notion means *a concept of or belief about something.*

So, we come into the marriage with baggage packed full of ideas or opinions that have no truthful foundation of God's word, and we form the concepts or beliefs that marriage or our spouses should be a certain way. And because of these misconceptions, you continue with the negative ways that you have. Since you haven't identified your negative behavior as baggage, you feel your spouse should adjust and not you. So instead of changing, you say, "This is just the way I am; you have to deal with it, or you can go."

The Lack of Knowledge

My people are destroyed for lack of knowledge: because thou hast rejected knowledge, I will also reject thee, that thou shalt be no priest to me: seeing thou hast forgotten the law of thy God, I will also forget thy children.
Hosea 4:6 KJV

Many people end up in divorce court that truly still love each other. That's because love all by itself doesn't make the marriage work. The Bible says, "My people are destroyed for a lack of knowledge." It is because we lack the knowledge that, in our ignorance, the enemy takes advantage. "The thief comes but for to kill, to steal, and to destroy..." John 10:10.

To show how the lack of knowledge can destroy us, I gave an example once during a Sunday Service. The example was while at a family picnic, a loved one had an acute onset of difficulty breathing due to an allergic reaction. The loved one's lips began to swell, the tongue began to swell, and hives broke out all over their body. Their skin color was changing, as well as they began to sweat profusely. Fortunately, a bag of medication was there that could help to relieve the loved one of these life-threatening symptoms. Inside the medication bag were Albuterol, Atrovent, Benadryl, Epi 1:1000, and Epi 1:10,000. So, I asked the congregation which drug of choice they would use to save their loved one. And no one was able to answer me. The reason no one could answer me is because of the lack of knowledge. No one had the knowledge to save their loved one, although the medication that was needed was there in a medication bag. Had they known the right drug was Epi 1:1000, given intramuscular could have saved their loved one, followed by Benadryl and nebulized treatment of Albuterol and Atrovent. They would still be with us. But ignorance was the killer.

The same goes for your marriage. Where you are ignorant, as it concerns marriage, you give the devil a place to destroy your relationship.

The Revelation on Doing Marriage God's Way

Jesus saith unto him, I am the way, the truth, and the life: no man cometh unto the Father, but by me.
John 14:6 KJV

I had a dear friend of mine, Pastor Vincent Robinson of Right Way Christian Center Church, come to my church on his Kingdom Wealth book tour. And that night, he asked the congregation a question on the above scripture. The question was, "What's the most important word in that verse?" For a few seconds, there was complete silence in the building. Then, a few of the saints attempted to answer the question. And to our surprise, his answer was the word "the." That's right, T.H.E - the. Pastor Robinson explained why that is; he said, " If the Lord had put "a" in front of the word "way" then that would mean that there is another way. But because the Lord used the word "THE," that means that He is the only way. After he explained that, the mental breakthrough light went off in my head. Married couples are getting married in Holy matrimony but are doing marriage another way, not God's way. And this is because of the baggage that was packed by someone else and the plain ignorance that is being brought into the marriage. In order to have a prevailing marriage, you have to learn how to do marriage God's way no exceptions.

*There is a way that seemeth right unto a man,
But the end thereof are the ways of death.*
Proverbs 16:25 KJV

One may say this seems like the right way to talk to my husband because I'm mad, this seems like the right way to treat my wife when she doesn't listen to me, and this seems like the right way to demean my spouse in front of people. Because it seems right doesn't make it right. Jesus said I am the way, so if you're going through some issues, find out the way to solve it. If you have some problems, find out the way to handle them. If your spouse is not loving, you right find out the way to correct it. If you're having disagreements, find out the way to agree. You have to learn what God says about things so that you can solve things the way. If you don't do marriage, God's way which is the way, you will end up with results you don't want. We all have baggage, yes, even you. When you first saw your spouse, what you saw was attraction, but you did not notice the baggage. You saw how beautiful she was, or you saw how handsome he was. There were numbers, notes, texts, or emails exchanged. Y'all hooked up, y'all had dinner, y'all went on dates, y'all had fun, but you never saw the baggage. That's because the baggage is in their minds, and their minds have been packed with pains, hurts, traumas, and all kinds of negative experiences. And with her beautiful self and with his handsome self, they brought the baggage into Holy matrimony with you.

This book of the law shall not depart out of thy mouth; but thou shalt meditate therein day and night, that thou mayest observe to do according to all that is written therein: for then thou shalt make thy way prosperous, and then thou shalt have good success.
Joshua 1:8 KJV

If you do marriage God's way, you will have a Prevailing marriage, and you will have 100% success.

Jesus answered and said unto them, Ye do err, not knowing the scriptures, nor the power of God.
Matthew 22:29 KJV

When you don't know what the Scripture says, you do error. So, if you don't know the scripture, that means you don't know the way, and when you don't know the way, you do a way that seems right. And that way, does not allow the power of God to bring the change you need into your marriage relationship. You can't change your spouse, but God can. You can't make a grown adult do anything that they don't want to do. And I think it's befitting to add this right here. You can't use violence and dominance to manipulate and control your spouse. That is abuse, and God will not be pleased.

Come unto me, all ye that labour and are heavy laden, and I will give you rest. 29Take my yoke upon you, and learn of me; for I am meek and lowly in heart: and ye shall find rest unto your souls.
Matthew 11:28-29 KJV

In the verse of scripture, we see the word labor. This labor does not refer to having a job. But Jesus is saying all that have been laboring and burdened with trying to live right but just don't know how. All that's trying to have a godly marriage, but just don't know how. He says come unto me, and I will give you rest. That rest means you've found the answer to what you're looking for. His way will remove the laboring and the burdens. To take his yoke means to allow His word to direct your life. To learn of Him means you're learning His word, you're learning about His benefits, and you're learning the way to have a prevailing marriage. God wants to take away the stress, struggle, and strain that you're facing. He wants to teach you and direct your life.

How Did We Arrive at This Place of Preconceive Notions?

It is an indisputable fact that everyone enters marriage with past hurts. When I say past hurts, I'm saying past negative experiences that have negatively impacted you. So, a past hurt can be negative information that has been placed in your baggage, negative past relationships, or negative examples of how to be married. These are all hurts that you bring with you in your baggage.

These past hurts cause destructive and negative behavior in husbands and wives. What makes it even more dangerous is that it is almost always justified as to why you behave the way you behave. Some say:

- You deserve this.
- I'm doing this because of what you are doing.
- This is just the way that I am. I was faking it while we were dating.
- This is normal. You just have the wrong expectations.
- There is nothing wrong with what I'm doing or not doing.
- You are just too sensitive.

What is in your baggage that is causing you to misbehave or think the negative way that you do? What causes you to act nasty, mean, and rude with no sympathy or empathy? What have you brought with you into your marriage?

What's in Your Baggage?

Past hurts; those negative things and experiences have been packed into your baggage. There are three basic categories of past Hurts.

- **A.** Parent hurts – iniquities, intervows, abuse, neglect, divorce, etc.
- **B.** Romantic hurts – rejection, betrayal, infidelity, hurtful words, divorce, abandonment, abuse, sexual abuse, etc.
- **C.** Life hurts – failure, serious illness, injury, financial problems, loss of loved ones, serious emotional or mental health problems, etc.

So here is why we need to get our past hurts healed. Hurts that go on unhealed hinder intimacy, they cause us to react to a spouse in extreme and unhealthy ways, and they cause a distortion of reality, in which we don't see the nature of our behavior and the problems that it's causing. We must deal with that hurts, or they will harm and even destroy our marriage.

How to Deal with Our Past Hurts Properly:

A. Be honest – face your fears and shame.
- No shame.
- No minimizing/acting tough.
- No expectations.

Anything in darkness is under the power of the devil. The light is God's domain.

> who hath delivered us from the power of darkness, and hath translated us into the kingdom of his dear Son
> **Colossians 1:13 KJV**

B. Claim – be responsible – admit your issues.

- Blame transfer was the original sin of marriage -

> And he said, "Who told you that you were naked? Have you eaten from the tree that I commanded you not to eat from?" The man said, "The woman you put here with me—she gave me some fruit from the tree, and I ate it."
> **Genesis 3:11-12 NIV**

- Don't justify your behavior because you believe your spouse is mostly the problem.

C. Forgive every single person in your past – including yourself.

- Forgiveness equals releasing them to God's judgment and refusing to judge or punish them for their mistakes.
- Unforgiveness is like an invisible umbilical cord that keeps us connected to and emotionally feeding from the negative people and places of our past.
- It doesn't matter how far in the past the bitterness goes – the people of your present will taste it the most.

- Your spouse will always pay the highest price for anyone you haven't forgiven -

** Blessing those who have hurt you is a secret to emotional and mental healing.

> *Bless them that curse you, and pray for them which despitefully use you.*
> **Luke 6:28 KJV**

D. Get help if you need it.
- Be humble and teachable.
- Go to church, talk to a leader, talk to your pastor.

Getting the help you need is not a sign of weakness. It is a sign of wisdom.

Chapter 3

Who Packed Your Baggage?

The original sin of marriage was blame transfer. And the most destructive spouses of those who come with baggage packed full of hurt and dysfunction, then blame others for their problems.

The reason a spouse would want to blame is to not take responsibility for their part or actions. When you don't deny it, it shows responsibility; it shows that you own the fact that something is going on inside of you that has been going on for years. You have been told this before, and you tried to correct the behavior, but it's short-lived. Then you find yourself right back in the pattern you thought was changed.

Who does this baggage belong to? Are you owning it? Will you claim It as yours?

Definition Time

Claim: to state that something is the case. To claim something is to own it, to take responsibility for it.

Responsibility: the fact of having a duty to deal with something, the state of being accountable, or to be blamed for something.

So, if I claim this mindset, that means I'm being responsible for its actions. I'm being responsible for the hurt it may cause others. I'm responsible for the negative words I say and the damage it may cause others. So, no longer can I say look what you made me do, but instead, I take responsibility for my behavior. Now, because of what has been packed into your baggage through the vehicle of your mind, you can potentially display behavior that provokes your spouse. Please remember that if you provoked something, you caused the reaction.

> *Fathers, provoke not your children to anger,*
> *lest they be discouraged.*
> **Colossians 3:21 KJV**

Provoked means "to arouse to anger," "a convulsion," or "a sudden outburst." Stimulate or give rise to (a reaction or emotion, typically a strong or unwelcome one) in someone.

According to the above scripture, it is possible that you can get a negative, unwanted reaction or emotion out of someone if provoked. Why, then, would you provoke your spouse? What's in your baggage? Did you cause that reaction? Yes or no? Are you going to own it or blame it? Well, you both have played a role in it. So, stop blaming and fix the problem. God does not hold us accountable for what someone might do to us. But He does hold us accountable for how we respond or react to what has been done to us. He also holds us accountable for provoking others to misbehave. That's why Scripture says not to provoke. So, Although you may have been provoked, your response is still your responsibility. If you want to see a change in your marriage, you both have to accept responsibility for the negative ways stored in your baggage. If you are in denial, you are trying to protect yourself from a truth that is too painful for you to accept at the moment. If you are responsible, you are accountable for your actions.

Own your baggage and claim it; it's okay. It's alright to say yes at times – times I cuss, yes at times I want to blame my spouse, yes at times I use my body to manipulate my spouse to get what I want, yes at times I shut down if I can't have my way, etc. You claim it; you own it; you say it's mine; I can admit I'm this way at times. I'm not going to be in denial; I take full responsibility.

Revelation from the Scripture on Accountability

3 Ways We See Accountability

God is looking for His children to be responsible and accountable to Him.

1. **Accountable to God**

Yes, each of us will give a personal account to God. So let's stop condemning each other. Decide instead to live in such a way that you will not cause another believer to stumble and fall.
Romans 14:12-13 NLT

Nothing in all creation is hidden from God. Everything is naked and exposed before His eyes, and He is the one to whom we are accountable.
Hebrews 4:13 NLT

You are responsible for your actions. When you own it, you are accountable to yourself. The greatest issue in marriage is your relationship with God. Your spouse should receive the overflow of your relationship with God, so when your spouse is having an out of baggage moment, instead of accusations, attitudes, and ultimatums, they receive from you the overflow of your relationship with God. So, how is your relationship with God?

2. **Accountable to Self**

Search me, O God, and know my heart; test me and know my anxious thoughts. Point out anything in me that offends you, and lead me along the path of everlasting life.
Psalms 139:23-24 NLT

3. **Accountable to Others**

The human body has many parts, but the many parts make up one whole body. So it is with the body of Christ. Some of us are Jews, some are Gentiles, some are slaves, and some are free. But we have all been baptized into one body by one Spirit, and we all share the same Spirit. Yes, the body has many different parts, not just one part. If the foot says, "I am not a part of the body because I am not a hand," that does not make it any less a part of the body. And if the ear says, "I am not part of the body because I am not an eye," would that make it any less a part of the body? If the whole body were an eye, how would you hear? Or if your whole body were an ear, how would you smell anything? But our bodies have many parts, and God has put each part just where he wants it.
1 Corinthians 12:12-18 NLT

Paul describes church members as members of one body, responsible for and accountable to each other.

- You can't conquer what you don't confront –

The story of David in 1 Samuel 17:1-51. We see where David took responsibility. He confronted Goliath, and he conquered the giant. We also see Caleb and Joshua In Numbers chapter 14 stand up, take responsibility, and say that they were ready to confront and conquer the giants.

You, too, when you take responsibility, can confront the baggage giant in your life and conquer what's been trying to conquer you. The giant of your mouth, the giant of your attitude, the giant of your demeanor, the giant of your anger, the giant of your tone of voice, and the giant of your blame game, etc. So, you claim it, you own it, you don't deny it, then you confront it and conquer it.

> *For every child of God defeats this evil world,*
> *and we achieve this victory through our faith.*
> **1 John 5:4 NLT**

Respect Your Spouse's Complaint

Every spouse has a right to complain, not to accuse. So, if your spouse is complaining to you about the way you're behaving, about the way you're treating them, about your attitude, about your tone, about your demeanor, and about the lack of getting their needs met. You should believe what your spouse is saying.

Especially when you know how you are, and you know how you can be, and you know the way you act at times. But when you're in denial, you go against the complaint, and you're ready to defend your attitude. Then you say things like you did it first, you shouldn't yell at me, you looked at me wrongly, etc. So, since the complaint was never addressed, we took our baggage to the grocery store, to family reunions, on vacation, and to church. Since you haven't had your mind renewed yet because you don't know how. It's best you listen, learn, and ask the Holy Spirit for help. **You must own it so that the Holy Spirit can Change it!!**

The Holy Spirit is our helper, and when we allow Him to come in, He can change us. People have tried to change their ways for years, leaning on their own strength and will. But willpower can only last so long under the constant pressure of temptation until it crumbles and falls. These negative ways have been packed in our baggage since childhood, from elementary school, middle school, high school, college, graduate school, clubs, family reunions, and into marriage. We've been carrying this baggage for years, decades, and presently. What's needed is the word of God enforced by the Holy Spirit to bring about the change needed in us.

4 Things That Shape the Way You Believe

Everyone who is reading the pages of this book thinks, behaves, talks, and reacts a certain way based on what was deposited in them. This is important that you understand because there are 4 things that shape the way you believe. This chapter is titled Who Packed Your Baggage? Remember, baggage is a metaphor for your mind. So, who packed the way you think, the way you behave, talk, and react into your mind? Now you know the way you are, so you're not denying it because you've taken responsibility. The question is, how did it get there?

The 4 things that shape the way you believe are your environment, credible others, repetitious information, and life experiences.

1. **Environment:** Your environment can be your home, where you spend most of your time, or where you were raised.

2. **Credible Others:** Credible others are people that you look up to, and that influence you.

3. **Repetitious Information:** Repetitious information is something that you hear on a consistent, ongoing basis. Or something that's been repeatedly told to you.

4. **Life Experiences:** Life experiences are those things that you have experienced in life, whether bad or good. What you experience shapes what you believe.

When you go to a new Dr., there's a lot of paperwork that you have to fill out. There are all types of questions that are asked that cause you to do a lot of recalling. After you're finished filling out the paperwork about yourself then, you have questions that you must answer about your family history. They question you about your family because they want to know what has been or can potentially be passed on to you. So, it is with what you believe. What you believe is the way you think. And that way of thinking has been passed on to you by your environment, credible others, repetitious information, and life experiences. In the environment I grew up in, I was exposed to violence toward women. I saw my father become violent towards my mother at a very young age. I saw my two older brothers, who had some of the most beautiful women in the world, become violent toward those beautiful women. Although I made up my mind at a young age that I wouldn't be like them. I still had that experience from that environment, from credible people to me who gave me repetitious information through their conversations and their behaviors. So, I have a family history of violence towards the opposite sex. Later in my life, although I said I would never be like them,

I was provoked to anger, and how did I respond? My response showed I had traits of my family history.

Why did I respond in the manner I did? Why did the traits that are distinguishing qualities or characteristics of my family history show up in my reaction or response? It is because they packed my baggage; they shaped the way I believe. My mind was preprogrammed and conditioned to respond in a negative way when provoked. The best teacher is experience, and because we have had bad experiences in the form of our past hurts. We now have a flawed way of thinking, reacting, behaving, talking, etc. And this flawed mind is what we brought over into our new marriage relationship.

What Gets to You First is Truth to You

What gets to you first is the truth to you. Even if it's a lying truth, it's still the truth to you because it got to you first. For example, if you tell a three-year-old child that black is red, they will grow up believing black is red. And because that was their experience, in their environment, from a credible source, they repeatedly heard it was truth to them. So, it becomes extremely hard to change their mind even after being exposed to what is the truth to them. Truth is the Word of God.

Sanctify them through thy truth: thy Word is truth.
John 17:17 KJV

Exposure to this information on truth doesn't bring the change. You're being exposed to the information by reading this book. The change comes when you get the information, the truth, and you embody it. In other words, you become an expression of that truth. You express the truth by living the truth, by talking the truth, by reacting the right way. When you respond or react negatively, you correct it and fix it, then come back the right way. Here's what the truth of God's Word has to say about the four things that shape the way you believe.

Environment

Wherefore Come out from among them, and be ye separate, saith the Lord, And touch not the unclean thing; And I will receive you
2 Corinthians 6:17 KJV

Blessed is the man that walketh not in the counsel of the ungodly, nor standeth in the way of sinners, Nor sitteth in the seat of the scornful. But his delight is in the law of the LORD; And in his law doth he meditate day and night.
Psalm 1:1-2 KJV

Credible Others

that ye be not slothful, but followers of them who through faith and patience inherit the promises.
Hebrews 6:12 KJV

Sanctify them through thy truth: thy Word is truth.
John 17:17 KJV

Repetitious Information

So then faith cometh by hearing, and hearing by the word of God.
Romans 10:17 KJV

that we should be to the praise of his glory, who first trusted in Christ. In whom ye also trusted, after that ye heard the word of truth, the gospel of your salvation: in whom also after that ye believed, ye were sealed with that holy Spirit of promise.
Ephesians 1:12-13 KJV

Life Experiences

This book of the law shall not depart out of thy mouth; but thou shalt meditate therein day and night, that thou mayest observe to do according to all that is written therein: for then thou shalt make thy way prosperous, and then thou shalt have good success.
Joshua 1:8 KJV

> *Practice these things, immerse yourself in them,
> so that all may see your progress.*
> **1 Timothy 4:15 ESV**

Who Told You You Were Naked

> *And the LORD God called unto Adam, and said unto him, Where art thou? And he said, I heard thy voice in the garden, and I was afraid, because I was naked; and I hid myself. And he said, Who told thee that thou wast naked? Hast thou eaten of the tree, whereof I commanded thee that thou shouldest not eat?*
> **Genesis 3:9-11 NIV**

In the Garden of Eden, there were many trees. The two trees that were named are the Tree of Life and the Tree of Knowledge of Good and Evil. And God told Adam, who then told Eve not to eat of the Tree of the Knowledge of good and evil. Adam and Eve were living the good married life; they were satisfied, and they were best friends living in the Garden of Eden. Eden was the original paradise, and they were living out paradise with each other. The word "Eden" refers to a place of pleasure, delight, and fulfillment. They received the blessing of the Lord.

Blessings are gifts from God that bring happiness to our lives. God also blesses us with his favor, empowering us to fulfill his plan for our lives. God blesses those who trust and obey him. God extends both spiritual and material blessings to those who follow him. Whatever Adam and Eve needed, it came from God, whether it was a material substance or knowledge. It all came from God. But when Adam and Eve ate from the tree that God commanded them not to eat from, the marriage changed. The blame game was introduced because of sin. That tree that was forbidden brought the opposite of the blessings to their union. The Paradise of Eden was destroyed by the prideful, rebellious choices of Adam and Eve. When they fell, they took God's ideal plan for marriage down with them. Now, this doesn't mean that couples cannot attain paradise; it just became much tougher to achieve. So God asked Adam the question, who told you you were naked? In other words, who packed your baggage? Who put this in your mind? Where did you get this way of thinking from?

Life is choice-driven. The quality of choice that you make determines the quality of life that you have. If you make bad choices, you get that way of living. If you make quality decisions, you get a quality life. And there has been bad negative information poured into your minds that keeps you making poor choices. Adam and Eve were never cursed, but because Adam and Eve made the bad choice to eat the forbidden fruit, their lives and marriages were drastically changed.

So, ask yourselves who told you to react that way. Who told you to keep secrets from your spouse? Who told you it's okay to have a sidepiece? Who told you to keep everything separate? Who taught you to disrespect your spouse? Who told you to lie to your spouse? Who told you not to have sex with your spouse if you don't get your way? Who told you to cuss out your spouse when you're angry? Who told you to act violently when disrespected? Who told you it's okay for you to break agreements that you have made together? God says I didn't teach you that. These lying truths that have been poured into your minds are the cause of poor decision-making. As a result of those choices, unnecessary toil, stress, struggle, and strain come into the marriage relationship.

Allow God to Teach You

You have to learn how to be married, and God wants to be your teacher. Because you have not been taught how to function in the most important human relationship on earth, disagreements, verbal fights, physical fights, separation, and divorce continue to occur. The Holy Spirit wants to teach you all things; he can even teach you how to be married, how to be a husband, and how to be a wife. You don't have to just survive in your relationship; your marriage can thrive. You do have victory already through Christ. There's nothing that the devil has done to you or your marriage that God cannot undo. There's nothing that has been stolen from you that cannot be restored. God can heal and forgive you for whatever you may have done to yourself and your marriage. Allow God's Word to teach you so that you can have a prevailing marriage.

But the Comforter (Counselor, Helper, Intercessor, Advocate, Strengthener, Standby), the Holy Spirit, Whom the Father will send in My name [in My place, to represent Me and act on My behalf], He will teach you all things. And He will cause you to recall (will remind you of, bring to your remembrance) everything I have told you.
John 14:26 AMPC

This book of the law shall not depart out of thy mouth; but thou shalt meditate therein day and night, that thou mayest observe to do according to all that is written therein: for then thou shalt make thy way prosperous, and then thou shalt have good success.
Joshua 1:8 KJV

Who Packed Your Baggage

See to it that no one carries you off as spoil or makes you yourselves captive by his so-called philosophy and intellectualism and vain deceit (idle fancies and plain nonsense), following human

> *tradition (men's ideas of the material rather than the spiritual world), just crude notions following the rudimentary and elemental teachings of the universe and disregarding [the teachings of] Christ (the Messiah).*
> **Colossians 2:8 AMPC**

Notice that the above scripture says, "See to it that no one carries you off or makes you captive by his so-called philosophy." And that is exactly what has occurred. You have been carried off by philosophy and man's ideas. Your minds have been held captive by the baggage placed in you from the plane nonsense that came from your environment, credible others, repetitious information, and your life experiences. And these "crude notions following the rudimentary and elemental teachings of the universe and disregarding [the teachings of] Christ (the Messiah)" have been brought into your marriage. This became truth to you, lying truth, of course, because it got to you first. You stick by it, swear by it, live by it. You may come down from a moment of anger, but you still have not changed your ways because the main issue in you has not been fixed.

The Baggage We Brought Into the Marriage

I have listed a few things, and obviously, this list may not contain every item in your baggage, but it gives you an opportunity to see some of the things that you bring into your marriage.

- Dividing everything into his and hers.
- Selfishness.
- Making your point, but you cut your spouse off from making their point.

- Don't respect your spouse's time.
- Don't listen to your spouse, but want them to listen to you.
- Your needs come first before your spouse's.
- You avoid responsibility.
- You like to take all the credit.
- Being secretive with your online activity/ cell phone activity.
- Putting your marriage on hold while you're raising your kids.
- My Kids come first.
- Giving each other your leftovers.
- Holding grudges and keeping score.
- Trusting your feelings more than your commitments.
- Secret stash.
- Making decisions without consulting your spouse.
- Mental Manipulation.
- Sexual manipulation.
- Sexual perversion.
- Threatening your spouse with leaving them to get them to conform to your ways.
- Stonewalling.
- Disrespecting your spouse.
- Miss-prioritizing your spouse.
- Not valuing your relationship.
- Running to Mama.
- Running to Daddy.

When I Choose to do the Marriage God's Way

Blessed is the man that walketh not in the counsel of the ungodly, nor standeth in the way of sinners, Nor sitteth in the seat of the scornful. But his delight is in the law of the LORD; And in his law doth he meditate day and night. And he shall be like a tree planted

by the rivers of water, That bringeth forth his fruit in his season; His leaf also shall not wither; And whatsoever he doeth shall prosper.
Psalm 1:1-3 KJV

This scripture, in retrospect, is, "cursed is the man that does walk in the counsel of the ungodly." And when your delight is not in the law of the Lord, you will not be planted, and the marriage doesn't prosper.

Little children, let no one deceive you. Whoever practices righteousness is righteous, as he is righteous.
1 John 3:7 ESV

It is said that practice makes perfect; I beg to differ. Because you can practice something the wrong way and learn how to do things in error. I would rather say perfect practice makes for a perfect performance. When you practice righteousness, you are intentionally doing it God's way. And God's way is the right way, the perfect way, "the way."

When I choose to do marriage God's way, I will have a prevailing marriage. His way will unpack the negative baggage that I brought into my relationship. His way will cause your thinking to prosper as a husband and as a wife, and you will prosper in your marriage.

Chapter 4

Unpacking The Baggage

During one of my counseling sessions with this particular couple, the wife stands up and says I'm just like my daddy. And she said it with such pride and conviction as if her disrespect towards her husband was justifiable because her daddy is that way. In her mind, based on what was packed in her baggage, she was behaving appropriately. I politely and lovingly told her, the reason you're wrong is because your daddy was wrong. The problem with the way your baggage is packed is that it could have been packed by good people with bad advice. So be careful who you take counsel from.

Not all advice is the right advice. Not all advice is sound. Every counsel that appears good may not actually be when subjected to the test of the Word of God. Therefore, be careful. Don't be in haste to follow every counsel. Sometimes, the people you respect because of their spiritual maturity, age, position, or relationship offer you the wrong counsel. If you follow the wrong counsel, you will bear the consequences. You may blame others, but it is useless passing the buck because the final decision rests with you, and blaming others does not change anything. God created marriage, so we must learn what God says about marriage so that we can do marriage in God's way. In chapter one of this book, I started with his and her baggage. Baggage, again, is a metaphor for the mind. Each person in the marriage relationship comes into the union of marriage with all kinds of negatives placed in their mind. And these negatives become the catalyst in the struggle to become one. And the same thing happens in your marriage relationship with Jesus. You are struggling to be one with His Word, walking in obedience. It is the church's responsibility to transform you through the Word of God. It is not your responsibility to transform the church. I had an experience with a young man in our church years ago. I was approached after church by this young man who told me that I should not be teaching on tithe and offerings. His reason was the people may not have it to give. This was a new convert who recently received salvation minutes before service ended, attempting to transform the church. This young man was working with ten minutes of salvation and trying to change the Word of God and the church.

Although he came to the altar, gave his life to God, and became spiritually alive, his mind was not renewed. All of the baggage he brought to church, that mindset left with him from the alter. In chapter two, if you recall, a past hurt is not just emotional pain but also negative thoughts placed in your head, negative behavior taught to you, and lies you've been told that you received as truth. These are the lying truths that have damaged your thinking, and you've brought those damaged goods into both marriage relationships—your marriage relationship with your spouse and your marriage relationship with Jesus. Please don't miss this: your marriage relationship with Jesus is of the utmost importance. And your spouse receives the overflow of your relationship with Jesus.

So, if that relationship with Jesus is not where it should be, in other words, you don't know him, or you just don't obey him. To not know Jesus and obey Him is to not know and obey His Word because they are one. And if you don't know the Word of God and you don't obey His word then your spouse and marriage could be suffering the consequences due to your ignorance and disobedience. If you don't know what the Word of God says, then how can you be obedient? Here's another thought for you. If you know what the Word of God says, how come you're not doing it?

> *If ye love me, keep my commandments.*
> **John 14:15 KJV**

> *Then said Jesus to those Jews which believed on him, If ye continue in my word, then are ye my disciples indeed*
> **John 8:31 KJV**

> *My people are destroyed for lack of knowledge: because thou hast rejected knowledge, I will also reject thee, that thou shalt be no priest to me: seeing thou hast forgotten the law of thy God, I will also forget thy children.*
> **Hosea 4:6 KJV**

What's Making the Decisions in Your Life?

What is causing you to continue to do negative things toward your spouse even when you know you should not be doing that? What's causing you to do the same thing over and over even when you know it's not the right thing to do? What's making the decisions in your life? What's packed in your baggage? You previously found out it was past hurts. Who packed the baggage? Well, that has to do with everything that you believed that you were exposed to. Here's a PowerPoint for you. Whatever has been accepted, settled, and set in you as a belief will control your life. In chapter 3, I shared with you four things that shape the way you believe. It is the negatives of your belief system that is impacting your life.

So, what shaped your beliefs? Your environment, credible others, repetitious information, and life experiences. And these beliefs are stored in your mind, and you bring that baggage into every relationship that you are involved in because it is your belief. There was someone or something in those four categories that influenced your decision-making. If you can, imagine you're standing at the altar about to say your vows to your soon-to-be spouse. You look amazing. For the bride, your hair, lips, and fingertips are all nicely done. You're looking as beautiful as ever in your wedding gown, smelling as if you've rolled on every flower in the Garden of Eden. And the groom is standing there. He is looking handsome and dressed very sharply. His hair is nicely groomed, mustache and beard are well-trimmed. And he has on his best-smelling cologne. What is not seen is all the baggage that you both have lugged to the alter.

All the past hurts, all the damaged parts of you, all the disappointments you've had, all the ugly, messy parts of you. The reason it's not seen is because the baggage is your mind. And it's that mindset that's carrying all the negative experiences of your life with you. You looked at the outer appearance. All you saw as a wife was how fine he was, how sexy he looked, the job he had, the money he made, and the car he drove. All you saw as a husband was how beautiful she was, how sexy she walked, how thick and healthy she was, and the way she smiled and made you feel. You had no idea of all the damage that was done to their thinking. You had no idea of what was deeply placed in their beliefs. Keep in mind what you believe is the way you will think, even if what you believe is a lie. So, when you moved in together – now that moving in can be before marriage for some if you keep it real, or after you became married, the principle is the same: what you saw them carry into the home was a suitcase you did not see the baggage in their mind. And after spending some time in the same living space, you begin to see the nice side and nasty side, the beauty side and the beast side. But what is making these decisions in your life for you to behave in such negative ways? When this part of you is corrected, you will be ready for the chapters to come.

The Lying Truth That Got to You First

When I was a young child, I was influenced a lot by my older brothers. And whatever they told me, that's what I believed. Living in the same house, I watched their behavior, the way they responded to girls, and confrontation. The way they talked and resolved issues. I heard and saw this repetitiously. They were credible to me, and their words were the truth to me. Although they may have meant well, they gave bad advises. And that advice was received as a lying truth and believed. And like the example I gave earlier about the child being told that black was red. What gets to you first becomes the truth to you, even if it's a lie. Here's how this applies to your marriage. You came into the marriage relationship with your own baggage of what is truth to you. Based on what you've been exposed to as truth, you also believe. Because of this baggage, you talk a certain way, behave a certain way, respond a certain way, etc.

In the process of becoming one, you tend to automatically block out things that are contrary to your belief system. So when issues surface, you feel your wrong is right, and so does your spouse. When in actuality, you're wrong. Therefore, what has been established in you about marriage in your belief system is controlling your life. Let me give you another example, if you were raised in a Christian Church. I'm pretty sure you know that Jesus died, and on the third day, he arose from the grave. If you heard someone say that Jesus is still in the grave, you would not believe that. Because the truth that he is risen got to you first. And it's hard for someone to change that truth that you were taught and believe. Now, just because some bad information got to you first, from your environment, credible other, repetitious information, and your life experiences, that doesn't make it the truth. It's only the truth to you because you believe it, and that affects the way you think.

A Revelation on Thinking

Why do you think the way that you do? The answer is it's because of the way that you believe. And what got to you first became truth to you, whether wrong or right.

Beloved, I wish above all things that thou mayest prosper and be in health, even as thy soul prospereth.
3 John 1:2 KJV

The soul of a man consists of the mind, will, imagination, intellect, and emotion. These five functions comprise one's thinking. So, this verse of scripture is saying you will prosper and be in health at the time and place that your thinking prospers. When you're thinking prospers, you prosper; when you're thinking prospers, your marriage prospers. Prosperity isn't just about money but also about you prospering in your thinking. In retrospect, if you're not prospering in your thinking, it's getting worse or remaining the same. So, the effects of what's been placed in your baggage that's impacting your thinking will show up in your marriage at some point. And this could be the cause of major issues in your marriage.

So How Do You Think?

Thinking is being able to look at a situation and gather information from that situation. Then you compare that to your core beliefs; based on your core beliefs, you make a decision, and the quality of the decision that you make determines the quality of the life that you live. Scenario: you're at the pool (husband) no one knows you. You see a few beautiful ladies wearing some really sexy bathing suits. The ladies are sitting around laughing while lounging. Your mind says there is no one here that knows you; your wife is not here. What surfaces now are your core beliefs. What's deep-seated in your beliefs is bad information from credible sources. And the credible source told you as long as the left hand doesn't know what the right hand is doing, you'll be fine. The left hand is your spouse. So, you thought about it and made the decision to approach the young ladies. After introducing yourself, one of the young ladies who happens to be your wife's supervisor says to you, isn't Monique your wife? Because of the husband's flawed core beliefs and erroneous decision-making, he has opened the door for the enemy to wreak havoc in his marriage. Flawed thinking derived from flawed core beliefs results in bad choices.

Flawed Core Beliefs

If your core beliefs are flawed, then you move further and further away from the life and marriage that God wants you to have and you desire to have. Because of these errored core beliefs, the husband continues to try to control and dominate his wife. And the wife continues to disrespect and rebel against her husband's headship.

What has been established in you as a belief will regulate your life? The deep-seated beliefs that you and I have about life, about marriage, about what a husband needs and the way he should be treated, about what a wife needs and the way she should be treated, actually control the way we behave with our spouse. It's in the becoming one where the struggles get real. You want to be one, but issues keep arising. Because you're applying the lying truth of your auntie, who said love doesn't pay the bills. You want to be one, but you are applying the lying truth of your favorite R&B singer who said it's good to have options. You want to be one, but you're applying the lying truth of your father, who told you to keep secrets from your spouse. You are applying the lying truth of your older sister who told you no money, no sex. You want to be one, but you are applying the lying truth of your older brother who told you if they don't obey, then slap them to conform. For the record, not all flawed core beliefs came from what you were told or heard but also from what you saw demonstrated. Because you saw flawed behavior and flawed reactions demonstrated by a credible person. You now mimic their flawed behavior and reactions in your marriage. Please also think about your children; they not only hear you, but they see you, too. One of the best things you can possibly do to help your children is to demonstrate to them what a good marriage looks like. Does your marriage look good in front of them?

Stored Beliefs

From birth, you have been storing information about what the world is like. In the world, it is marriage, finances, behavior, the treatment of others, etc. You have built your own version of what a marriage should be, a relationship should be, and the treatment of a spouse when they get you upset should be, and we have established that as truth. We then evaluate everything based on what we have come to believe is true. The quality of our marriage and what we accomplish in marriage will then be determined by the validity of the Stored beliefs. Here is an example: if you have ever used GPS, you know that you can drive, and it will show you where you currently are as you drive. But when you type in coordinates or the address to where you want to go, it will show you an overview as well as show you how to get there. Now, if you go to the same destination on a later date, all you have to do is look at the previous address traveled. The GPS will pull the destination information back up and take you back to a place you've been. Why is that? Because you've programmed the GPS. What you've programed is stored in there and will come up when triggered.

If you have stored in your core beliefs that leadership equals controlling and dominating your wife, then that's what you'll do. If you have stored in your core beliefs that cutting your husband off while he's talking and then out-talking him is okay because you believe that this strategy will help you make your point. Then, you will continue to disrespect your husband. As a child, you've been programmed with methods, behaviors, reactions, and ways that have been stored in you. Positive and negative experiences are stored inside of you. How do you know what to go to and what to stay away from? It's because you've had an experience that has stored information on that specific experience in your beliefs.

Led by the Flesh

For I know that in me (that is, in my flesh,) dwelleth no good thing: for to will is present with me; but how to perform that which is good I find not.
Romans 7:18 KJV

Another translation reads this way.

For I know that nothing good dwells in me, that is, in my flesh. For I have the desire to do what is right, but not the ability to carry it out.
Romans 7:18 ESV

The flesh is your sinful nature. As long as we live in the flesh, there is a sin opportunity present. Now, this is not an excuse to continue to live a sinful life but to recognize when your flesh is trying to lead you. Your Flesh wants what it wants because it's selfish. The verse says your will to do right is present with you, but yet you continue to do the opposite. Why is that? What's making the decisions against your will? When you receive the answer and then apply the principles, you will begin to see and experience the change of having a prevailing marriage.

We Must Practice Righteousness

Now, just because I live in my flesh, and there is no good thing that dwells in my flesh, doesn't give me the right to indulge in a sinful lifestyle. So, you have to deal with the lie that was given to you and received by you as truth. And some have stored the lie that "once saved, always saved, so I can live whatever lifestyle I choose to." This lying truth is proven to be wrong by scripture and, therefore, must be eradicated and removed from your minds.

BAGGAGE CLAIM

Little children, let no one deceive you. Whoever practices righteousness is righteous, as he is righteous.
1 John 3:7 ESV

You must intentionally and purposely practice living right. When I say right, I'm saying living a righteous lifestyle. Again, you can practice something the wrong way because it was taught to you or demonstrated to you in the wrong way. And because you have practiced doing it the wrong way for so long, you have now perfected doing it wrong. Perfect practice makes for a perfect performance. So, I must intentionally practice the righteous way of living. If you don't practice doing marriage God's way, which is the right way, you will continue on a failing path. When you make up your mind to live a righteous life on purpose, you are then allowing the Word of God to perfect those things that concern you.

A Deeper Look

For I know that good itself does not dwell in me, that is, in my sinful nature. For I have the desire to do what is good, but I cannot carry it out. For I do not do the good I want to do, but the evil I do not want to do—this I keep on doing. Now, if I do what I do not want to do, it is no longer I who does it, but it is sin living in me that does it. So I find this law at work: Although I want to do good, evil is right there with me. For in my inner being, I delight in God's law; but I see another law at work in me, waging war against the law of my mind and making me a prisoner of the law of sin at work within me - Romans 7:18-23 NIV.

For I delight in the law of God, in my inner being
Romans 7:22 ESV

As we take a deeper look at what's making the decisions in your life, we see in the above scripture that there is a struggle going on with the will and the flesh. A conflict between the desire to do good and the inability to carry it out. Although in your inner being, your spirit man, you delight in the Word of God. Yet there is a war being waged against your mind, making you a prisoner to disobedience. This is all at work on the inside of you. In the scripture below, we see what is required to receive Jesus Christ as your Lord and Savior. We first see Romans 10:9-10, and then we read Romans 12:2. Of course, if we read in order, Romans 10 is before Romans 12. What's the significance of my sharing this? It's because Salvation takes place before mind renewal. When you receive Jesus Christ as your Lord and Savior, the only thing that happens is you become spiritually alive Romans 10. Your mind is still the same because your mind has not yet been renewed. So, your thinking is still the same; some, if not all, of your ways are still the same. The way you respond, react, behave, and talk are still the same. You brought your selfishness into your marriage relationship with Jesus and the marriage relationship with your spouse. The lust of the flesh, the lust of the eyes, and the pride of life are all selfishness. Yes, at the altar when you receive Jesus Christ as your Lord and Savior, you brought baggage with you.

The same thing happened when you said your I do with your spouse; you brought baggage to the altar. The reason is that you had not been transformed in your thinking when you got married to Jesus and to your spouse. You got married but were still with the formation of the world system or ways of doing things. Your mind had been saturated with ungodly counsel, lying truths, and negative ways prior to marriage. You came into the church spiritually ignorant, not knowing the truths in God's Word. So, when you heard the truth in the Word of God, it went against your flawed core beliefs. What the preacher said to you became distasteful because your flesh did not want to do it. The same thing happens in your marriage when your spouse asks you to minister to their sexual need, and you don't feel like it. It's now a distasteful situation for you, and you reject their need for sex.

that if thou shalt confess with thy mouth the Lord Jesus, and shalt believe in thine heart that God hath raised him from the dead, thou shalt be saved. For with the heart man believeth unto righteousness; and with the mouth confession is made unto salvation.
Romans 10:9-10 KJV

….And be not conformed to this world: but be ye transformed by the renewing of your mind, that ye may prove what is that good, and acceptable, and perfect, will of God.
Romans 12:2 KJV

For all that is in the world, the lust of the flesh, and the lust of the eyes, and the pride of life, is not of the Father, but is of the world.
1 John 2:16 KJV

Shot Caller

What's making the decisions for your life? What's calling the shots? Earlier in this chapter, I shared with you lying truths that got to you first, a revelation on thinking, flawed core beliefs, stored beliefs, led by the flesh, we must practice righteousness, and we took a deeper look at what doesn't takes place when you receive Jesus as your Lord and Savior. So where are all the lying truths you received and believed stored? Now, let's put all this together, and I will reveal to you what's making the decisions and calling the shots in your life.

God is so awesome, and He does everything well! He designed us in such an amazing way. We are powerful creatures engineered by God.

> *I will praise thee; for I am fearfully and wonderfully made: Marvelous are thy works; And that my soul knoweth right well.*
> **Psalm 139:14 KJV**

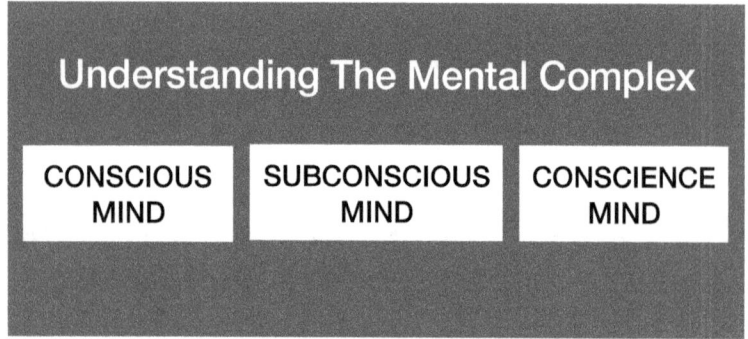

Understanding The Mental Complex

CONSCIOUS MIND	SUBCONSCIOUS MIND	CONSCIENCE MIND

God has engineered us to have a conscious mind, a subconscious mind, and a conscience. The conscious mind is designed to decipher and decide whether something is truth, fact or not, and believable or not. The subconscious mind serves as the place of stored truths and autopilot to the conscious mind. The conscience is your belief system. There are four things that shape the way you believe. I have covered these earlier, but for emphasis's sake, I will review them again.

First, your social environment shapes what you believe. If you are in a social environment of poverty-minded individuals who have no hope of prospering, you can be impacted to believe the same way that you'll never prosper.

Secondly, repetitious information. What you hear consistently shapes the way you believe. If you've heard consistently on an ongoing basis, you're going to be just like your daddy, a womanizer, an alcoholic, or just like your momma, chasing men, their money, and never knowing who your child/children's father is; if that's all you heard repeatedly, you will believe that.

Thirdly, credible other people that you look up to who are influential to you. Whatever they say to you becomes truth, and it shapes the way you believe wrong or right.

Fourth is life experiences. When you experience something significant, that event shapes what you believe. So when faced with that event again, you will know what to do or not to do. That experience made you a believer. Here is the process of God's engineering at work. I will use myself for this example. My conscious mind is alert and aware, then it receives information, and it deciphers whether it is the truth or fact. Now, because the information that's being received is coming from a credible person on a repetitious basis in the social environment in which I live, I'm experiencing the truth acted out in front of me. My conscious mind says its truth. Information that you choose to agree with, through a conscious effort, becomes truth to you. Then, my conscious mind passes the deciphered truth over to my conscience, which is my belief system. So now the information is believed because it was received through one or all of the vehicles that shape the way I believe. My subconscious mind now stores this information as truth. Your subconscious mind is amoral, neither good nor bad. Its function is simply to carry out its task of assessing your belief system standards and acting in agreement with it. It is your subconscious that is keeping you locked into a belief system. This is the shot caller and the decision-maker of your life. Although the function of the subconscious can have good intent, its decisions may not always be in your best interest. Allow me to explain if somewhere along life's path, you accepted something that was a lie as truth (because you really thought it was the truth at the time), you misinformed your belief system. So now your subconscious mind (autopilot) has locked in on the information that is not true, but it thinks it is. The result of this can be your subconscious mind operating and directing your life in agreement with something that is not true. For example, a young boy, from the time of adolescence to becoming a young man, was told that a man is to dominate and control his wife. That a wife should do as she's told and provide financially and sexually for him. Because this was received by the conscious mind as truth, his subconscious mind locked in on that lying truth and automatically guided him in accordance with what he believed as true. Having this lie stored as baggage, he gets married and responds to his new wife in accordance with what he believes is the truth. Now, issues ensue in his marriage because the shot caller, the decision maker, his subconscious mind is making the decisions for him in his marriage. Then, one day, while attending The Prevailing Marriage conference, he heard the Word of God on marriage. He heard scripture like:

Husbands, love your wives [be affectionate and sympathetic with them] and do not be harsh or bitter or resentful toward them.
Colossians 3:19 AMPC

Husbands, love your wives, as Christ loved the church and gave Himself up for her.
Ephesians 5:25 AMPC

Likewise, ye husbands, dwell with them according to knowledge, giving honour unto the wife, as unto the weaker vessel, and as being heirs together of the grace of life; that your prayers be not hindered.
1 Peter 3:7 KJV

After seeing the scripture and hearing the Word of God, he is now aware that what he was taught is not true. Even though he now knows the truth from God's Word, his subconscious mind will not automatically release those old lying truths. Just as a reminder, I call a lie a lying truth because you were told a lie that you received and believed as the truth. So, he is unable to replace the lie with God's truth. Here is why. The subconscious mind (auto pilot) is strong and too consistent to be easily changed. The subconscious mind continues to operate and direct your life by the old lying truth until properly instructed to release the old and lock on to the new information. You will continuously remain in this pattern of hearing and knowing the real truth but be subconsciously misguided by the old information until you know how to replace and assimilate new truths in your belief system. The lying truths that are stored in your subconscious mind are the baggage that you bring into your marriage. These lying truths that are triggered by words, recalled by images, and stirred up by emotions will continue to be the decision maker for your life. The negative ways you respond, react, behave, and talk are subject to the (shot caller) subconscious mind. These errored ways and lies that you believe are the right ways will be automatically recalled when triggered. And you will behave in accordance with that flawed way despite knowing the righteous way.

Transforming the Mental Complex

```
TRANSFORMING THE MENTAL
         COMPLEX

  CONSCIOUS    SUBCONSCIOUS     CONSCIENCE
     MIND          MIND            BELIEF

                              INFO  INFO  INFO  INFO
```

The way you think is the way you believe, and the way you believe is the way you will respond, react, and behave. If these ways are flawed and in error, then they must be removed and corrected. From your childhood, you could have been negatively conditioned and programmed in error by people who may have meant well and loved you, but nonetheless still in error. These flawed ways must be eradicated. Earlier, I shared that when you received Jesus as your Lord and Savior, you became spiritually alive, but your mind remained the same. So, you will think and behave the same way you did prior to receiving salvation. The reason is your mind has not yet been renewed, so transformation has not yet taken place.

Although you are a new creation, you still function by the old man and his ways. Because you have not had your mind renewed, you subconsciously do the wrong things. You love the way you love because that's how you've been taught. And if you were taught that you love your spouse based on how well they performed, then you were taught in error. If you were taught that you don't have to secure your wife, then you were taught in error. If you were taught that you only have sex when you feel like it and not when your spouse does, then you were taught in error. If you were taught that your husband doesn't need to be respected; he's not your daddy, then you were taught in error.

Another thing God did not design us to be led by what we feel. He said, "Set your affection on things above." That means we are in control of our emotions. Wives, you have sex more than you feel. Husbands, you talk more than you feel. Yes, sex drives may be different, and that may be factual for you. His libido may be higher than yours. But your libido doesn't trump the scripture; you still are supposed to render due benevolence. These negative ways and lying truths stored in your baggage must be removed.

> *And be not conformed to this world: but be ye transformed by the renewing of your mind, that ye may prove what is that good, and acceptable, and perfect, will of God.*
> **Romans 12:2 KJV**

We see that the above scripture says not to be conformed to this world. That means do not act in accordance with the rules, ways, and standards of the world. What's in the world? Selfishness and disobedience, that's the world system. And these worldly ways are the baggage that needs to be removed from your subconscious mind. In order for you not to be conformed to your old ways, you have to be transformed in your thinking. The way your thinking is transformed is your mind has to be renewed. When your mind is renewed, transformation takes place. Then you are no longer in formation to negative, flawed ways of the world. In an earlier chapter, I shared with you that whatever information gets to you first becomes truth to you. This can be a major problem in your transformation process. If the information that you received was negative, when new information comes, your subconscious mind rejects it. This is because the new info goes against what was first received in your belief system. So, although you know it's the truth, it's hard for you to accept it. Then what must I do to get rid of the initial negative information to accept the truth, you might ask? You turn to God. Since God designed us, what does he say to do? We see the answer in the scripture.

> *This book of the law shall not depart out of thy mouth; but thou shalt meditate therein day and night, that thou mayest observe to do according to all that is written therein: for then thou shalt make thy way prosperous, and then thou shalt have good success.*
> **Joshua 1:8 KJV**

> *But his delight is in the law of the LORD; And in his law doth he meditate day and night.*
> **Psalm 1:2 KJV**

Notice how both verses of scripture say to meditate day and night. God is telling you how to change you internally. Which in turn will eventually cause the transformation needed. You are being instructed on how to retrain your internal programming mechanisms to change you so that you effectively unpack the lying truths stored in your baggage.

If Your Core Beliefs are Flawed

If your core beliefs are flawed, you have to retrain yourself, reprioritize your marriage, and reprioritize your spouse based on the truth of God's Word—the way this is done is to discipline yourself to be consistent. Discipline is enforced obedience. You set an obtainable goal, and that goal should be to better yourself to better your marriage. And you use discipline to stay consistent at it. To better yourself, you have to unpack the stored lying truths. This can be done by disciplining yourself to stay consistent in saturating your mind with the Word of God. Saturation of the Word of God will remove false truths and flawed core beliefs from your subconscious mind. When you hear and receive God's Word, you are receiving God's doctrine. The doctrine is God's order or ways of doing things. God's Word will reprove you, that is, to remove your erroneous ways of thinking and doing things. His Word will correct you. After your errored ways of thinking have been eradicated. The Word of God will assimilate the truth in you. Teach you what you need to do that's correct or the right way. The Word of God will teach you how to systematically apply what you have learned from the scripture. In other words, give you righteous instructions. When your mind is renewed, the shot-calling decision-maker of the subconscious mind becomes the truth from God's Word.

So then faith cometh by hearing, and hearing by the word of God.
Romans 10:17 KJV

"All scripture is given by inspiration of God, and is profitable for doctrine, for reproof, for correction, for instruction in righteousness:"
2 Timothy 3:16 KJV

Chapter 5

New Mind

I want to start this chapter with a reminder that baggage is a metaphor for the mind. So far, you have read about your old ways derived from an old mindset. And in chapter four, you read how to unpack that baggage. Now, we focus on the renewed mind from the truth of God's Word so that you have a mind for a prevailing marriage.

> *And do not be conformed to this world [any longer with its superficial values and customs], but be transformed and progressively changed [as you mature spiritually] by the renewing of your mind [focusing on godly values and ethical attitudes], so that you may prove [for yourselves] what the will of God is, that which is good and acceptable and perfect [in His plan and purpose for you].*
> **Romans 12:2 AMP**

In order for you to be transformed, you have to have your mind renewed (made new again). To be made new again, you need truthful information. Because of the old negative mindset, you thought, reacted, and behaved in ways that may have been offensive to your spouse. But when those flawed ways are eradicated, new truths can come in to take their place. Another thing to mention is that transformation could have taken place in your life because your mind was renewed in a specific area. But in other areas like marriage, a renewed mind is still needed. So, there is still a struggle in various areas of your marriage because transformation has not taken place. Since the mind has not yet been renewed, the thoughts, behaviors, and reactions remain the same. Although you may say you'll change, that becomes the pattern of promises made but only lived out for a short term. This is because when the mind is not renewed, a stronghold may be at work in your life. A stronghold is a mental thought pattern that has not been broken. It's a spiritual fortress made up of negative thoughts. These mental strongholds are fortified dwelling places where demonic forces can hide and operate. In a nutshell, it's a way of thinking and feeling that has developed in you a life of its own. It could be a pattern of lying, cheating, watching porn, or displaying anger with violence. These are strongholds at work in the lives of many married people, but with God's help, not anymore. I must mention again you need to have your mind renewed in order to be transformed.

Learning to be Married

You are not born with the automatic knowledge of being a great spouse. You have to learn how to be married and how to become one. Marriage is two selfless servants serving each other. But until your mindset is changed, you are still a selfish spouse who wants what they want, when and how they want it. Everything is me and mine. Now, this may not be for all areas of your marriage, but selfish ways can poke their heads up when triggered if the transformation has not taken place. You have to learn how to be married and how to become one. This should take place through God's Word directly from the scripture or from someone who is able to share God's Word, godly advice, and experience on marriage with you.

Marriage is God's idea. He is the originator of marriage. It is His precepts that you should govern your marriage by. God made the first man, Adam, and the first woman, Eve, and they became one flesh.

That is why a man leaves his father and mother and is united to his wife, and they become one flesh.
Genesis 2:24 NIV

Christ wants to teach you.

"Come unto me, all ye that labour and are heavy laden, and I will give you rest. Take my yoke upon you, and learn of me; for I am meek and lowly in heart: and ye shall find rest unto your souls."
Matthew 11:28–29

Have you ever found yourself saying I'm getting so tired of this? You've been saying the same thing over and over to your spouse but are not seeing any change. Your spouse says that they'll change, but a day or week later, those negative marriage-altering ways cause you to become so frustrated with them again. And you just feel so tired, you're at wit's end, and you don't know what else to do. Then this is your scripture; listen to the voice of the Lord as he speaks through this verse. He says, "Come unto me all ye that labor and are heavy laden." He's saying if you are laboring to find the answer, looking for a way to bring change to your marriage, searching for understanding and peace but can't find any, and your marriage issues are mentally and emotionally wearing you out. You are feeling heavy-laden. Jesus says He will give you rest. That rest is the peace you are searching for and need. And that rest will come from Him because He has and is the answer. He says, " Take my yoke upon you". In other words, like a yoke on oxen that the farmer uses to direct the oxen. Jesus says take my yoke. In other words, allow me to direct your life. "And learn of me." Let me teach you the way; my way is the only way. He's saying He will teach you His way in every area of your life, including how to be married. Jesus and his Word (the Bible) are one. He says, " I'm meek and lowly in heart." He will love you through whatever you're going through as you are learning what you need to do as a spouse. " And ye shall find rest unto your souls," so no more stressing and worrying but praying and believing with a righteous resolve. Resolve is the spiritual disciplined strength of mind to obey through delays, hardships, and adversity without wavering in faith until the promises you're believing for manifest. Let's look at this verse in another translation for even greater clarity.

"Come to Me, all who are weary and heavily burdened [by religious rituals that provide no peace], and I will give you rest [refreshing your souls with salvation]. Take My yoke upon you and learn from Me [following Me as My disciple], for I am gentle and humble in heart, and YOU WILL FIND REST (renewal, blessed quiet) FOR YOUR SOULS.
Matthew 11:28-29 AMP

You have to learn His way, which is the way from the Word of God. And the Word of God will teach you how to have a prevailing marriage by doing marriage His way. We see in the below verse what you should do to prosper and have good success in your marriage. God is saying here to keep speaking his Word despite what you may be facing, meditate, that is, see the end result of God's Word on the canvas of your imagination day and night, and also do what he says that's written in the Bible. Then you'll make your way. God is saying you are responsible for making your way prosperous and successful. "Your way" is any righteous thing you may be involved in, like a business venture or even your marriage. "You will make your way" your marriage prosperous and successful. So don't just say it, don't just imagine it, but also do what the Word of God says.

> "This book of the law shall not depart out of thy mouth; but thou shalt meditate therein day and night, that thou mayest observe to do according to all that is written therein: for then thou shalt make thy way prosperous, and then thou shalt have good success."
> **Joshua 1:8 KJV**

Will Power

When living a godly life, you can't depend solely on willpower to help you when temptations of the old you try to resurface. Will power only last for so long before it crumbles under the constant pressure of temptation. When Jesus was led into the wilderness to be tempted (tested or tried) by the devil, he did not rely on His willpower.

Of the three times that was recorded of Him being tempted, He relied on the Word of God. It was the Word of God that kept Him from failing or falling for the test of the devil. He resisted the devil by using what was written, and the devil left him alone. You don't resist the devil in your own might but in the power of the scripture.

When you use the Word of God and resist the devil, his test, and temptation to get you back into your old ways, he will flee from you as well.

> "Then was Jesus led up of the Spirit into the wilderness to be tempted of the devil. And when he had fasted forty days and forty nights, he was afterward an hungred. And when the tempter came

to him, he said, If thou be the Son of God, command that these stones be made bread. But he answered and said, It is written, Man shall not live by bread alone, but by every word that proceedeth out of the mouth of God. Then the devil taketh him up into the holy city, and setteth him on a pinnacle of the temple, and saith unto him, If thou be the Son of God, cast thyself down: for it is written, He shall give his angels charge concerning thee: And in their hands they shall bear thee up, Lest at any time thou dash thy foot against a stone. Jesus said unto him, It is written again, Thou shalt not tempt the Lord thy God. Again, the devil taketh him up into an exceeding high mountain, and sheweth him all the kingdoms of the world, and the glory of them; and saith unto him, All these things will I give thee, if thou wilt fall down and worship me. Then saith Jesus unto him, Get thee hence, Satan: for it is written, Thou shalt worship the Lord thy God, and him only shalt thou serve. Then the devil leaveth him, and, behold, angels came and ministered unto him."
Matthew 4:1-11 KJV

"Submit yourselves therefore to God. Resist the devil, and he will flee from you."
James 4:7 KJV

You don't Have to Carry that Baggage Any Longer

"giving thanks unto the Father, which hath made us meet to be partakers of the inheritance of the saints in light: who hath delivered us from the power of darkness, and hath translated us into the kingdom of his dear Son:"
Colossians1:12-13 KJV

"and giving joyful thanks to the Father, who has qualified you to share in the inheritance of his holy people in the kingdom of light. For he has rescued us from the dominion of darkness and brought us into the kingdom of the Son he loves,"
Colossians 1:12-13 NIV

There is an old saying where I grew up and it's "You can take a person out of the projects, but you can't take the projects out of the person." That saying does have some truth to it. The above verse of scripture says, "Who hath delivered us from the power of darkness." On a Sunday morning during a church service, as I was teaching my message, I asked a young man sitting amongst the congregation where he was from. And he replied from West Palm Beach. I asked the young lady sitting next to him where she was from, and she said Tampa, Florida. Now, keep in mind that my church is in Tampa, Florida, and we are at my church while I'm asking the members these questions. I then asked the young lady where are you now? She said Tampa, Florida. I proposed to her another question. I asked if you are currently in Tampa, Florida; how can you be from Tampa, Florida? Because if you're from somewhere, you are not currently there. Then, all the eyes in the congregation just opened up wide like a deer staring at the headlights. I could hear the chatter all over the auditorium saying that's true. I never thought of it that way.

If you look at the above scripture again, it says, *"Who hath delivered you from the power of darkness."* That means you're not there anymore. When you received Jesus Christ as your personal Lord and Savior, you were delivered from the power of darkness. And not just delivered but brought into the kingdom of light. That means you are not there anymore, so you don't have to live by its lies, deceptions, and manipulations. The NIV translation says," *For he has rescued us from the dominion of darkness and brought us into the kingdom of the son he loves."* You don't have to carry that baggage any longer. Back to my old saying, "You can take a person out of the projects, but you can't take the projects out of the person." You can receive salvation and be brought into the Kingdom of the son he loves but still think like you are in the projects under the (power of darkness). And that's because you are present in the body in the kingdom, but your mind is still in darkness. No transformation has taken place because your mind has not yet been renewed. I want you to understand that darkness has no control over you; you're in love under new management.

There are two more old sayings that I would like to share to make my emphasis clear. The second saying is, "It's not where you are from; it's where you're at." You can come out of darkness into light but still think like you're in darkness. The same question I asked the church that Sunday morning I now ask you. Where are you from? And where are you at? Your answer should be you're from the power of darkness, but you are now in the kingdom of the son he loves. The third old saying is, "When in Rome, do what the Romans do." You may not be in Rome to do what they do, but the principle remains the same. You're no longer under the dominion of darkness but have been brought into the kingdom of light. Since you're not in Rome and you're not in darkness any longer, but now are in the light. You have to do what Kingdom citizens of the light do. They put on the mind of Christ.

Put Off the Old Man

I want to share a personal experience that I had as an example to help your understanding regarding the old man. While at a picnic with family and friends, some confusion amongst friends erupted. Other family members and friends got involved quickly to de-escalate the situation. I then heard certain individuals say, "That couldn't have been me 5 years ago. The old me would have cussed them out." Another said, " yea, I agree because the old me would have punched someone in the face". Then, it dawned on me that something in these particular individuals had changed about their ways based on their confessions. They both said, "The old me". What was even more surprising was they were both back in an environment where the old man, with his old way, was accustomed to being. However, they refused to allow the old man access back into their lives. When I later questioned these two people about why they didn't respond and react the old way. Their answer was pretty much the same. They said they had been changed; they had given their lives to the Lord years ago. No more immature responses and behaviors because their minds had been renewed. They had made up their minds to put off the old man with his deeds. And you, too, have that choice. You don't have to pull out the old ways from your baggage and then act out in a negative way.

You are now in the kingdom of light; you can choose to put off the old man. Get rid of his ways, throw them out of your baggage (mind). And intentionally put on and walk in the new man now placed in your baggage (mind). You're being taught God's way to do marriage, so choose to walk in that knowledge. Not your old ways where you'd lie to your spouse, keep secrets from your spouse, deceive your spouse, control your spouse, financially manipulate your spouse, sexually manipulate your spouse, belittle your spouse, reject your spouse, cuss out your spouse, punch your spouse, verbal abuse your spouse, sexually abuse your spouse, stone wall your spouse, not secure your spouse, and disrespect your spouse. But walk His way, talk His way, respond His way, behave His way, live His way, and do marriage His way. You can put off the old man.

> *"...And you will make your way prosperous
> and have good success."*
> **Joshua 1:8**

New Mind

"Lie not one to another, seeing that ye have put off the old man with his deeds; and have put on the new man, which is renewed in knowledge after the image of him that created him:"
Colossians 3:9-10 KJV

"that ye put off concerning the former conversation the old man, which is corrupt according to the deceitful lusts; and be renewed in the spirit of your mind; and that ye put on the new man, which after God is created in righteousness and true holiness. Wherefore putting away lying, speak every man truth with his neighbour: for we are members one of another. Be ye angry, and sin not: let not the sun go down upon your wrath: neither give place to the devil."
Ephesians 4:22-27 KJV

When you don't handle marriage problems in God's way, you give place to the devil. And that's exactly what he wants a way in. Satan wants to get back into your old closet, thumb through your old wardrobe (ways), and redress you in your old man. Now you find yourself responding harshly to your spouse the old way you used to. Saying things like, Don't talk to me, don't touch me, you are so dumb, the stupidest thing I ever did was marrying you, etc. These ways ought not to be. " Be angry, and sin not." If the Word of God is telling you to be angry, then that emotion is ok. But not to sin because you're angry; then sin is not ok. So, then, God has to teach you the right way to handle anger so you don't sin. Let's read the right way.

Let no foul or polluting language, nor evil word nor unwholesome or worthless talk [ever] come out of your mouth, but only such [speech] as is good and beneficial to the spiritual progress of others, as is fitting to the need and the occasion, that it may be a blessing and give grace (God's favor) to those who hear it. And do not grieve the Holy Spirit of God [do not offend or vex or sadden Him], by Whom you were sealed (marked, branded as God's own, secured) for the day of redemption (of final deliverance through

Christ from evil and the consequences of sin). Let all bitterness and indignation and wrath (passion, rage, bad temper) and resentment (anger, animosity) and quarreling (brawling, clamor, contention) and slander (evil-speaking, abusive or blasphemous language) be banished from you, with all malice (spite, ill will, or baseness of any kind). And become useful and helpful and kind to one another, tenderhearted (compassionate, understanding, loving-hearted), forgiving one another [readily and freely], as God in Christ forgave you.
Ephesians 4:29-32 AMPC

New Garments

"I delight greatly in the Lord; my soul rejoices in my God. For he has clothed me with garments of salvation and arrayed me in a robe of his righteousness, as a bridegroom adorns his head like a priest, and as a bride adorns herself with her jewels."
Isaiah 61:10 NIV

God is saying now that you have received my son Jesus as your Lord and Savior, you are now spiritually alive. And I have clothed your spirit man with the garments of salvation and arrayed your spirit in a robe of righteousness. This Robe of righteousness is something that only God can provide for you. When Jesus died for you, He clothed you in his righteousness. You no longer have to live in the shame of your past ways. When God sees you, He sees the arrayed righteous robe of Christ. You've been dressed in the finest of robes! Don't put on your rags again! Let him dress you and fill you. Wear His righteous robe well. For He is truly merciful and graceful, abounding in love and faithfulness.

The question is, do you wholeheartedly see yourself as clothed in a beautiful robe of the righteousness of Christ? Or do you still define yourself by your weak moments or the shame from your past? Your physical man may look the same, but when God looks at you, you're sharply dressed, decked out with new garments.

> Listen to me, O royal daughter; take to heart what I say. Forget your people and your family far away [let go of your past shame]. For your royal Husband delights in your beauty; honor Him, for He is your Lord.
> **Psalms 45:11–12 NLT**

Don't Just Dress the Part Live the Part

> "No one sews a patch of unshrunk cloth on an old garment, for the patch will pull away from the garment, making the tear worse. Neither do people pour new wine into old wineskins. If they do, the skins will burst; the wine will run out and the wineskins will be ruined. No, they pour new wine into new wineskins, and both are preserved."
> **'Matthew 9:16-17 NIV**

Now, in this new relationship with God, you've come out of the kingdom of darkness and are no longer under its dominion. Your mind is being renewed, and transformation is in progress. You're saturating your spirit with the Word of God day and night. And your flawed core beliefs are being eradicated. God is doing something fresh and new on the inside of you. He's getting rid of the old unclean heart and creating in you a new one. The above verse of scripture talks about new wine in old wineskins. An old wineskin has stretched to its limits, and placing new wine in the old skin will cause it to tear at the seams. This is because the new wine will expand, and the old wineskin has no more elasticity or room to expand. The old wineskin will burst because it's unable to carry the new wine. In other words, Christ wants to do something new in you, and your old mind can't receive it or understand it.

The wine represents the Holy Spirit that Christ wants to pour into your new wineskin. Allow the new wine (Holy Spirit) to help you with living the transformed life in Christ. It's no more you that live, but Christ that lives on the inside of you. Now that you're dressed in Christ's robe of righteousness, the Holy Spirit will help you to stay dressed in it. So, when you are facing troubling martial situations, the Holy Spirit keeps you dressed in your right mind (righteous mind). There was a man in Luke 8:35 of the Bible who was possessed with many demons. Jesus cast out those evil spirits from that man. And when they found the man, he was sitting next to the feet of Jesus cloth, and in his right mind. Now, if Jesus can cast demons out of people and cause them to be in their right minds, surely, if you stay seated at his feet (submit to His way), He will keep you clothed in your new spiritual robe of righteousness and keep you living the married life with a renewed mind.

And people came out to see what had happened. They came to Jesus, and found the man from whom the demons had gone out, sitting at Jesus' feet, clothed and in his right mind (mentally healthy); and they were frightened.
Luke 8:35 AMP

Do you not know that your body is a temple of the Holy Spirit who is within you, whom you have [received as a gift] from God, and that you are not your own [property]?
1 Corinthians 6:19 AMP

Can You Forget the Old Way Your Mind Ways Dressed?

> *Brethren, I count not myself to have apprehended: but this one thing I do, forgetting those things which are behind, and reaching forth unto those things which are before, I press toward the mark for the prize of the high calling of God in Christ Jesus. Philippians*
> **3:13-14 KJV**

So, you don't have a sea-like God that you can cast your old mind into and never remember the negative ways again. All the old ways that your environment, credible others, repetition, information, and life experiences stored in you.

> *He will turn again, he will have compassion upon us; he will subdue our iniquities; and thou wilt cast all their sins into the depths of the sea.*
> **Micah 7:19 KJV**

Then how can you possibly forget like Paul did and walk in the new garments? It's by choice. You have to choose to pull down every thought that goes against the Word of God. Every thought that tries to come to the forefront of your mind, you have to intentionally pull it down and leave it behind you. That's the old you and its old ways, but the new you don't live by those ways anymore. Forgetting it is not allowing those thoughts to stay in the front of your mind. The past is behind you. So, you pull those thoughts down by choosing to use God's Word over those thoughts that try to reclaim the throne of your mind. It's an intentional and on-purpose effort. Don't grant permission to the past negative impartations. You don't give them the power to take over your renewed mind in Christ. Also, you don't cosign with the past negative thoughts by speaking in agreement with them.

Therefore take no thought, saying....
Matthew 6:31 KJV

(for the weapons of our warfare are not carnal, but mighty through God to the pulling down of strong holds;) casting down imaginations, and every high thing that exalteth itself against the knowledge of God, and bringing into captivity every thought to the obedience of Christ
2 Corinthians 10:4-5 KJV

Once you realize that you're in control, you don't have to allow errored thoughts that don't line up with the word of God to stay in your mind. If you replace those thoughts with God's word, you are well on your way to achieving good success.

"Roll your works upon the Lord [commit and trust them wholly to Him; He will cause your thoughts to become agreeable to His will, and] so shall your plans be established and succeed."
Proverbs 16:3 AMPC

Marriage is Work, so you must work at marriage. It's not easy, but it's very rewarding. The word of God says that if I commit my works to Him, that could be any work, but since this book is about marriage, we're talking about your marriage work. God will cause your thoughts about marriage to become agreeable with His Will. The Will of God is His plans, guidance, strategies, and instructions for your life and your marriage. As a result of your thoughts agreeing with His thoughts. Your plans for your marriage will be in alignment with His Will (plans) and become established and succeed when you embrace God's presence and honor His plan for you as a spouse. Your marriage will be successful. Remember, God walked with Adam and Eve in the Garden of Eden until they rebelled.

Chapter 6

Breaking the Habits of Bad Baggage Packing

During a Sunday morning service at my church, I taught an illustrated message. On the stage, I had a set of luggage, the smallest being an average-size carry-on suitcase and the largest being the average size for a large suitcase. During that message, I asked the congregation a question. The question was if you were going on a 3-night 4-day trip by yourself, which suitcase would you pack to take with you? Several different answers were given that morning. But the number one answer was it boiled down to how many items you wanted to bring and the way you packed your baggage. The answer I gave was I would take the average-size carry-on. If it were my wife traveling, she would need our entire luggage set. The carry-on was free for me, but for my wife, she would have to pay additional costs for all the extra baggage. And that was my exact point: when you are carrying unnecessary weight with you as you travel along the journey of marriage, It can cost you greatly. All because of your bad habits of baggage packing.

Again, I must reemphasize that the baggage is a metaphor for the mind. So, if you have a bad habit of allowing negative thoughts to be packed in your mind or you repack them by recalling your old ways, your marriage will always pay the price.

In order for you to break these bad habits of baggage packing, your effort must be intentional.

> *For a dream comes with much business and painful effort, and a fool's voice with many words.*
> **Ecclesiastes 5:3 AMPC**

The dream, the desire that you have for your marriage, is going to require you to handle the business of marriage and put in the required work. Your dream marriage is going to take much purposeful effort.

Intentional means *to be done on purpose; to be deliberate. You have to have on purpose, deliberate effort to help the dream manifest.*

- You have to be intentional about the way you treat your spouse in a loving and affectionate way.
- You have to be intentional about thinking positively about your spouse and stop negative assumptions.
- You have to be intentional about not being selfish and consider your spouse. Marriage is not all about you.
- You have to be intentional about communicating in a loving way to your spouse.
- You have to be intentional about meeting the needs of your spouse.
- You have to be intentional about not shutting off when your spouse has an opinion different from yours.

- You have to be intentional about apologizing and assuming responsibility for being in the wrong.
- You have to be intentional not to be a control freak.
- You have to be intentional not to take your spouse for granted.
- You have to be intentional about putting in the effort to make your spouse smile.
- You have to be intentional about listening to your shortcomings from your spouse. Your spouse has the right to complain to you about the way you're making them feel.
- You have to be intentional about not accusing your spouse. But you can share how they are making you feel.
- You have to be intentional about walking in agreement.
- You have to be intentional about doing marriage God's.
- You have to be intentional about having a prevailing marriage.

You have to be intentional about these efforts, so you break the bad habit of baggage packing.

The Habitual Offender

The reason why most spouses are not able to do things intentionally in a positive way is because they have become habitual offenders, having a mental stronghold. We normally hear the habitual offender terminology as it concerns criminal activity. But you can also be a habitual offending spouse because a spouse can repeatedly do the same things that offend relationships.

The definition of **habitual** is *done or doing constantly or as a habit.*

The definition of an **offender** is *a person or thing that offends, does something wrong, or causes problems.*

So, you can be habitually causing issues in your marriage, you can be habitually disrespecting your spouse, you could be habitually rejecting your spouse, you could be habitually dishonoring your marriage, you could be habitually not doing marriage God's way. Now, if you go back to chapter four, where you read about the mental complex. And I shared with you there that you could receive new information but continue to do things the same old way. Allow me to share another example. Your wife tells you that you make her feel like a child when you talk down to her. Or your husband says you make him feel disrespected when you talk to him in a manly tone. Remember, what got to you first is what you believe. So what you received as the way things should be done may be wrong. But because you believe that way is right, it becomes truth to you. Despite you hearing the truth of God's Word on "Be angry and sin not," "Let not the sun go down on your wrath," and "A soft word spoken turns away wrath." You endure with this new information for a short duration, then find yourself right back to your old ways. If this describes you, then you have the ways of a habitual offending spouse. You constantly, as a habit, do things that are wrong, cause problems, and offend your spouse and your marriage.

Beloved, I wish above all things that thou mayest prosper and be in health, even as thy soul prospereth.
3 John 1:2 KJV

What is the soul of man (human)? It's your mind, will, imagination, intellect, and emotion. These five things comprise your thinking. The scripture above reads, "Even as thy soul prospereth." That "even as" is saying at the place and time that your "soul" (thinking) prospers or is (changed or renewed). A prosperous soul is a renewed mind. The success of your mental prosperity is dependent upon the Word of God. As a result of your thinking prospering, because of a renewed mind, everything else is prosperous, including your marriage. In retrospect, if your mind is not renewed, you will not prosper in your thinking because you will continue to habitually offend. Until you get your mind renewed, become transformed, live in the new garments, receive the new wine (Holy Spirit) in the new wineskin, and use the Word of God to pull down every thought that tries to hold you back. You will continue to have a habitually offensive lifestyle. Even after you and your spouse have talked about it, argued about it, read books on it, and sought counseling regarding it, you continue to do those offensive things. You continue to lie about money, keep secret credit cards and secret money stashes, reject your spouse sexually, be flattered by the opposite sex, entertain the conversation of the opposite sex, cheat, stonewall, manipulate, and deceive your spouse. Until you've had your mind renewed and your soul prospers, you will continue to do the same thing over and over again.

Your Will and Your Feelings

The will of man (human) has to do with your ability to choose. You have the right to set the criteria on what you will believe or will not believe; you have the right to choose what you will do or will not do. You've been designed by God that way. He will not force you or make you choose. And the criteria you use to determine what you will come from your core beliefs. Living your new life with Christ as a believer, your core beliefs should be based on the Word of God. God does have a plan for your life, and the plan of God is seen in the Word of God (The Bible). When you hear the Word of God, you get the Will of God for your life. The Will of God is God's plans, strategies, guidance, instructions, directions, and answers for your life. Your will as a believer in Christ should be to do the Will of your Father God. The way this is done is for you first to hear the Word of God because faith begins where the Will of God is known. Secondly, you need to trust the Lord and lean not to your own understanding. Your ways from your understanding will cause you to get what you've been getting, which obviously, you didn't like those results if you are reading this book. Living according to His Will (plan) will get you the results God has planned for you to have. Thirdly, you have to commit your works to God. Your work is really anything that you are trying to accomplish and become successful at. I shared earlier that marriage is work, so you should also commit your marriage work to the Lord as well. The reason this is so important is that God will cause your thoughts to become agreeable to His Will (plan) for your life. You will begin to know God's plan and live in agreement with it. The result will be a successful prevailing marriage.

Lean on, trust in, and be confident in the Lord with all your heart and mind and do not rely on your own insight or understanding.
Proverbs 3:5 AMPC

For I know the thoughts and plans that I have for you, says the Lord, thoughts and plans for welfare and peace and not for evil, to give you hope in your final outcome.
Jeremiah 29:11 AMPC

Roll your works upon the Lord [commit and trust them wholly to Him; He will cause your thoughts to become agreeable to His will, and] so shall your plans be established and succeed.
Proverbs 16:3 AMPC

Your will gives you the drive and determination, but your will does not keep you constant. To understand this, look at how most people start out their new year. Most start with the will to be in better shape, so they buy all the workout gear and join the gym. The first few days or a couple of weeks look pretty promising. The drive and determination were there because of their will. But before the month was out, their attendance began to drop off to the point that they eventually stopped working out. What happened? They had the clothes, gear, membership, and the will. But with all that, they were still missing an extremely important component to accompany the will. Please understand your will can stop and give up. Your will does not form habits. This is why in Matthew chapter 4, Jesus used the Word, not His Will, habitually against satanic assaults. But what made Jesus steadfast, unmovable, being habitual (constant) with God's Word?

You Woke Up Like This

The bad habits that you may have in certain areas of your life didn't just happen last night for you. You woke up like this. What? Yes, since you were a child, you have been placed in the formation of the world by the four things that shaped the way you believe. Again, they are your environment, credible others, repetitious information, and life experiences.

> *Behold, I was shapen in iniquity;*
> *And in sin did my mother conceive me.*
> **Psalm 51:5 KJV**

The word iniquity, in its original Hebrew, means to be twisted, crooked, or bent. So, they are crooked ways about you that were passed on by those factors that shape the way you believe. Again, what you believe is the way you think. The way you think is the way you'll react, respond, and behave, even if those ways are twisted and bent. These are factors that shaped your personality. It is because of what you've been around, seen, and heard that has contributed to the way that you function. So, if you have children, they're learning how to be married by watching and listening to you. You are the best demonstration and model of a marriage for them. They're watching how you both react, respond, and behave towards each other. So, will your children learn from you God's way of doing marriage? Or will they be bent, twisted, and destroyed by you? What are some bad habits you woke up with and could possibly be passing on? The bad habit of devaluing your spouse, taking them for granted, not meeting their needs, blaming them for everything wrong with you, making excuses, not prioritizing them, not taking responsibility for your wrongdoing, etc. You woke up like this. This doesn't make you a bad person; it just means you've learned some bad ways along life's journey. And the way you conquer this bad habit is with discipline. Discipline is what's needed to accompany your will. This is what Jesus used to remain constant in doing the will of God.

saying, Father, if thou be willing, remove this cup from me: nevertheless not my will, but thine, be done.
Luke 22:42 KJV

Even in a vulnerable moment for Jesus when His Will to continue was being challenged. He used discipline to keep His will doing God's Will. Discipline is enforced obedience. Discipline is what's needed to be consistent. Your will gets you started, but discipline keeps you constantly going and doing. You have to be disciplined in doing the opposite of bad habits to habitually do God's Will for your life. This is why Holy Spirit is so important. He will help you, teach you, and guide you in all truths and understandings. It is the holy spirit that will reveal to you what the mind of God is for your life.

If ye be willing and obedient, ye shall eat the good of the land
Isaiah 1:19 KJV

Then said Jesus to those Jews which believed on him, If ye continue in my word, then are ye my disciples indeed
John 8:31 KJV

Your will can get you to agree to God's Will. In other words, you know you should live God's way, and that's your will to do that. But it takes discipline to habitually obey His Will.

You have to remain constant by discipline to form a habit. It is said that it takes 21 days to form a habit. Now, why is this different from the will? Because will can give up. Your will gets you started. However, discipline will cause you to remain constant in doing what you set out to accomplish. And when you remain constant at allowing God's word to correct bad habits for 21 days, you form a new habit. What is taking place is your mind is being saturated with new truths from God's words. Bad habits are being erected, and new positive, godly habits are being formed. This is great because you are literally being transformed because your mind is being renewed. So, you will no longer be in formation with the old ways. And your spouse begins to experience the new you. This is a celebratory moment because it is like a fresh new marriage all over again. Even if you've been married for 10, 20, 30-plus years, you too can have a prevailing marriage. How? By doing marriage God's way.

You're In Control of Your Emotions

Let not your heart be troubled: ye believe in God, believe also in me.
John 14:1 KJV

The Bible says, " Let not." That alone means that you are in control. You have to be able to allow or not allow your feelings to direct you. Your feelings come from your emotions. Your emotions are part of your thinking. Your thinking must prosper in order for other areas of your life to prosper, which includes your marriage. Emotions are not bad. God has designed them to alert us as to how we should feel in certain situations and environments. Your emotions should alert you, but not control you. I was once at the funeral of a person that I did not even know. I went to support a friend. Of course, at a funeral, your emotions tell you that you should feel sad. So, I noticed that I started feeling sad, and I found myself tearing up. I said to myself wait a minute now. You don't even know the deceased person. And I immediately changed the way I was feeling by changing my thoughts. I took control of that emotion that alerted me to feel said. I said no to that feeling. Why? I'm in control, and I chose not to live sad in this moment because of my feelings. I "Let not my heart be troubled." And you can, too.

You don't have to go with your feelings. You are in control and can go against the grain of those emotions. You can intentionally interrupt that feeling by doing the opposite. That action of opposing your emotions is called an emotional interruption. In marriage, many times, women don't feel like having sex. Men don't feel like talking. You have to interrupt those feelings because you have to minister to the needs of your spouse. You both agreed to meet each other's needs. Wives, you interrupt those emotions and have more sex than you feel. And husbands, you interrupt those emotions and talk more than you feel. You are in control, not your emotions. Now, you have to use discipline to do this. It requires enforced obedience.

The Way God Designed You

God designed you to go towards pleasure and to stay away from pain. Have you ever burnt your hand on an iron? You know now, because of the pain you experience, to be careful when using the iron. Why? You want to stay away from that painful experience. Also, other painful experiences like touching a hot stove top or slamming your hand in a door. Those painful experiences make you instinctively stay away from it. You've also been designed to go towards pleasure. The things that bring you delight. The reason why you continue to treat your spouse wrong as a habitual offender, even after hearing their complaint, hearing the truth of God's Word, and receiving counseling, is because of inconsideration and no empathy. When you're sympathetic towards a person, that means you feel sorry for them. But when you are empathetic, that means you can relate to them because you have been in that situation before yourself. So, if you can't relate to your spouse, you have to learn to use empathetic hearing. In other words, you put yourself in their shoes and try to see things from their perspective. But when you are a habitual offender, you're always inconsiderate in your reactions, responses, and behaviors. You have no empathy. You're indifferent, detached, insensitive, unconcerned, disinterested, dismissive, and cold.

You're just not concerned in your heart with the way you're making them feel.

The Pain You Caused

When you choose to do wrong, offensive things to your spouse and cause all kinds of marital problems, you are literally inflicting pain on your spouse. When you lied, you caused pain; cheated, you caused pain, stole money, you caused pain, had an affair, you caused pain, put your children against your spouse, you caused pain, put your parents in front of your spouse, you caused them pain. The pain that you allow in your marriage from your wrong ways can cause divorce, separation, mental torment, and anguish. Married couples must understand that when they get married and become one, a merger takes place. The mindset of a spouse has to be one because of the merger. The language of the merger is.

When you look good - **I look good.**
When you feel bad - **I feel bad.**
When you look bad - **I look bad.**
When you feel good - **I feel good.**
When you hurt - **I hurt.**
When you have pain - **I have pain.**

The pain of your spouse becomes your pain. And by God's engineering, you've been designed to stay away from pain and go towards pleasure. So, you stay away from the painful things you use to inflict on your spouse. And move towards the pleasure you cause them to have by doing marriage God's way. You have to equate sin to pain because the devil has disguised sin as pleasure. The devil is a liar and the father of lies. And sin will also lie to you.

choosing rather to suffer affliction with the people of God, than to enjoy the pleasures of sin for a season
Hebrews 11:25 KJV

So, when you make your spouse's pain your pain, that should cause you to stop offending, treating them wrong, and causing issues in your marriage. You must form habits of meeting your spouse's needs, have emotional interruptions, and do more than you feel. This will require your will to commit to doing this, coupled with discipline and consistency to achieve it.

Chapter 7

Guard Your Heart Protect Your Mind

Be sober [well balanced and self-disciplined], be alert and cautious at all times. That enemy of yours, the devil, prowls around like a roaring lion [fiercely hungry], seeking someone to devour.
1 Peter 5:8 AMP

After 911, the game changed for air travel and baggage. In the airport, you often hear announcements to keep an eye on your baggage. Watch out for suspicious packages and baggages left alone. TIA has driven home the point to all travelers to watch out for terrorists trying to destroy more lives by putting something destructive into someone else's baggage. They were training travelers to be on the lookout, on guard, and not to be a doorway for the enemy. There have been many marriages wrecked and lives and families destroyed because of a doorway being open to sin. And that doorway is the mind, simply by the spouse accepting and entertaining the negative intrusive thoughts of the enemy. The scripture instructs us to be sober, alert, and cautious at all times. This is so important to understand because your enemy, the devil, is always looking for a way into your life to devour you. Even if your mind has been renewed and transformation has taken place, satan still prowls around, seeking a way back into your life. He wants the right to your mind to control your thinking. But you must not give him access, guard your heart, protect your mind, and protect your marriage.

Be On Guard

> *Above all else, guard your heart,*
> *for everything you do flows from it.*
> **Proverbs 4:23 NIV**

One of my favorite sports to watch is boxing. In the sport of boxing, it is taught a good defense sets you up to have a great offense. You would hear the trainers say time and time again to keep your guard up. The referees say at the beginning of the fight to protect yourselves at all times. The words of the trainer and instructions from the referee are critical to the fighter's success during the fight. And it is also critical for you as a spouse to guard your heart at all times. In Hebrew, guard means to keep above all keeping. So, above anything else, you guard – your marriage, family, bank account, passwords, your car, or your house. Be sure to guard your heart with more vigilance than anything else. If the heart is not guarded, the marriage is not protected. The heart I'm referring to is not the four-chambered muscle in the center of your chest. But the seat of man, your spirit-man, the one you really are. The doorway is an entry and exit point. And to corrupt the heart, Satan likes to gain access through the eyes, ears, mouth, and mind. So, as a spouse, you have to be aware of your surroundings and Satan's M.O. Modus Operandi, which is the way someone functions or works as a habit. Your adversaries, the devil, likes to use your eyes to focus on the forbidden, your ears to hear the negative, your mouth to speak his lies, and your mind to be in doubt. This is how he causes a spouse to keep secret sins, be unbelieving, and always focusing on the negatives in their marriage. When you stand guard, you keep the bad out of the heart, and you allow the good in.

The Bible is a book of wisdom, and the book of proverbs tells you how to handle some of life's situations and how to deal with people who may be easy or difficult to get along with. King Solomon wrote Proverbs 4:23, and he was the wisest man who ever lived, a man of great wisdom. Solomon realized that what you do flows from who you are. That's why he instructs Israel to guard the heart (who you are) because the wellspring of life (what you do) flows from it. This is why it is essential for you to guard your heart because if you don't, you will be who Satan wants you to be and not who God wants you to be in your marriage. What you do as a spouse in your marriage is because of what you have allowed to enter into your heart. Remember, you are no longer the old you, and you don't have to be led by your old ways.

Protect Your Mind

above all, taking the shield of faith, wherewith ye shall be able to quench all the fiery darts of the wicked.
Ephesians 6:16 KJV

Fiery darts are those intrusive thoughts that the devil uses to invade your mind. His objective is to get you into doubt and unbelief. See, if doubt is not checked while it's in your head, it will progress to the heart. Then, the doubt unchecked becomes unbelief. So, you have to protect your mind by not allowing those corrupt thoughts to stay there. If you allow those negative intrusive thoughts of Satan to linger, rumination will take place, and you'll find yourself thinking long about what's wrong and not right with your marriage. Thoughts that are contrary to the word of God you must take captive. How is this done?

By taking responsibility for the thoughts, you allow them to stay and go.

By using God's Word to combat those contrary thoughts. By choosing to focus your thoughts on things above and not beneath.

By saying faith-filled confessions daily. Speaking in agreement with what God has already said.

By mediation. Seeing the end results of God's Word on the canvas of your imagination.

casting down imaginations, and every high thing that exalteth itself against the knowledge of God, and bringing into captivity every thought to the obedience of Christ
2 Corinthians 10:5 KJV

The devil wants you to focus your thoughts on the negatives about your spouse and marriage. He wants you to keep score, so he frequently accuses your spouse to you, causing you to reminisce on how they may have hurt you or wronged you. You have to be willing to pull those devilish thoughts down. Although those things may have happened, you're choosing to move forward. And just like you've used your faith for clothes, the crib, and cars. You use your faith for your marriage, and you use your faith for yourself as a spouse. You are not who the devil says you are, you are not what you did, you are not the mistake of your parents. You are a child of the Most High God. And when you do marriage His way, your marriage will prevail.

Don't Cosign with the Devil

Negative intrusive thoughts, if not checked and pulled down, will eventually come forth from your mouth. Satan (diablos) loves to accuse because he's the accuser of the brothers. He loves to put bad thoughts in your head about your spouse so you can say them in agreement with him. He wants you to say you married the wrong person; he wants you to say he's a terrible husband; he wants you to focus on all the things they have ever done wrong. He wants you to believe that your marriage is a failure and that there's no hope for it. He wants you to say this marriage is over; I'm done. He wants you to say your wife is stupid and belittle her. He wants you to say all she does is disrespect me. He wants you to say all the wrong things about your spouse and your marriage every day. Because he knows if you do, you will have what you say. So Satan puts those negative thoughts in your head so you can cosign with him regarding your marriage. But the devil is a liar. You don't have to cosign with the devil anymore. You are now guarding your heart and protecting your mind. So, instead, you say what God has said about your spouse and your marriage. You speak to where you want your spouse to be, not where they are.

Release Your Faith

For with the heart man believeth unto righteousness; and with the mouth confession is made unto salvation.
Romans 10:10 KJV

Now, what you are about to read, your spouse may not be there yet, but you release your faith over your spouse and marriage. Remember, faith is released by your mouth. For example, you say this about your husband. You're the best husband in the world; you give good love, you secure me, you are a great leader, a faithful husband, an amazing provider, an awesome communicator who is open and honest. For example, you may say this about your wife. You are an affectionate wife, a loving wife, a kind, caring wife; you respect me at all times, you give good love, and you satisfy my sexual needs. You're my best friend and cheerleader. You're speaking to where you want your spouse to be, not where they are. But satan wants you to take the thoughts he puts in your head about your spouse and marriage and say that. Satan did not create marriage, but he tries to destroy it. Speak in agreement with the scripture, and watch God work in your marriage.

Therefore take no thought, saying, What shall we eat? or, What shall we drink? or, Wherewithal shall we be clothed?
Matthew 6:31 KJV

Chapter 8

A New Mind Repacked

Stand fast therefore in the liberty wherewith Christ hath made us free, and be not entangled again with the yoke of bondage.
Galatians 5:1 KJV

Now that your mind has been renewed and your flawed core beliefs have been reproved, you can now effectively think like a spouse whose mind has been renewed. Married women...you cannot have the mindset of a single woman, attend a single woman's committee to get advice on your marriage only to get advice on what "they would do if they were you" for you to then take that bad counsel back to your house and allow it to tear your house down. Married men...you cannot have the mindset of a single man where you are present physically but emotionally distant. Having a mind that can't articulate how to meet her greatest needs but can demonstrate your anger very well. In order to be the transformed spouse, you must think like a spouse who does marriage in God's way.

I Love Me Some (Him)

> *We love him, because he first loved us.*
> **1 John 4:19 KJV**

To effectively walk in your transformation thinking like a spouse with a renewed mind. You must first understand what the greatest issue in marriage is. That issue is your personal relationship with God. Marriage is God ordained covenant created by God. And when you honor God's plan for marriage, you will achieve the marital success you desire. It was because He loved you first despite your conditions in life that caused your hearts to be able to love. Regardless of your past mistakes, ungodly lifestyle, and sin, He still loved you, but not the sin. And it is His example of love that reminds us of time and time again that you should love others. And one of the others is your spouse. Let's look at another text.

> *If ye love me, keep my commandments.*
> **John 14:15 KJV**

Here is the acid test for all who say they love God. Jesus says here, "If you love me, you will obey me." In other words, you display your love for God by your disciplined obedience to His Word. When you first came to God, you didn't love Him. You had not spent enough time with the Lord to love Him. To be honest, most people came to Him when they found out all He could do for them. Some say, "He can get me into heaven; sign me up!". Others say, "He can heal my marriage; sign me up!". So, people came to receive Jesus as their Lord and Savior because of the benefits. But when you begin to spend time with Him and get to know Him, you begin to see how good He's been to you. And because of the time spent with Him, you begin to love you some Him. The beauty in this is that because of the love relationship you have with Jesus, your spouse gets the overflow of that relationship. So even when your spouse may have upset you or caused you disappointment, remember how good God was to you when you weren't deserving, when you were disobedient; when He woke you up in the middle of the night to pray and you did not; when you forgot to give God the praise after blessing you with your request for a promotion. Your spouse should get the overflow of that relationship. And you love them anyhow, serving them with love and a smile.

Two Selfless Servants

"But he that is greatest among you shall be your servant."
Matthew 23:11 KJV

Your marriage should be two selfless individuals happily serving each other. The reason for your service to each other is so important is because you have 100% of what your spouse needs. You come together as one to meet each other's needs. And when needs go unmet, this becomes an open-door opportunity for the devil to have access to your marriage. To the devil, a selfish spouse is a welcome mat saying, "Come right on in." Your attitude while serving should also be of the utmost importance because it shows you are willing and lovingly providing the highest quality of service. If you can imagine that you are at an extremely upscale fancy restaurant, the building is all arrayed in marble and custom stonework. The greeters are all color-coordinated and wear the biggest, warmest smile. Live musicians are playing the latest smooth jazz, and the ambiance is just right. However, the server is very unprofessional, impatient, and not familiar with the menu and the environment at all. Your food arrives late and cold, all while the server is displaying a poor attitude. All throughout the building, the ambiance, the musicians, and the greeters were all great. However, the quality of service you received ruined the evening and what could have been an experience of a lifetime. All because of the type of service that was rendered. I use this as an example to indicate that top-quality service is vital. I'm sure you would not want terrible service like the one mentioned in the example. So, treat your spouse like a customer and say, "Let me serve you up." Render the best quality service that you can possibly provide to your spouse.

Most people think that because they believe that they are great, they should be the ones waited on. But the Lord looks at greatness differently. He said if you are the greatest, then your greatness should be displayed in your service. In putting others 'interests above your own. In laying down your life to help your spouse, care for your spouse, and to build up your spouse. Did you know that Jesus even washed the feet of His own disciples? I'm telling you that you can't get any greater than that.

> *After that He pours water into a basin, and began to wash the disciples' feet and to wipe them with the towel wherewith he was girded.*
> **John 13:5 KJV**

Serving your spouse shows them that you care for them. To care means you are anticipating their need before they even ask. It shows them you are thinking about them. To effectively meet your spouse's needs, you have to respect their differences. God uniquely designed the male and female to have different needs. And when those differences are accepted and respected, the marriage thrives. However, when the differences are rejected, issues begin to surface. Men and women have all kinds of needs. But the four greatest needs of a man are respect, sex, friendship, and domestic support. The four greatest needs of a woman are security, open, honest communication, leadership, and non-sexual touches. When you are serving each other and meeting needs, you leave no room for outsiders to come in.

Let's Talk About Sex

Let the husband render to his wife the affection due her, and likewise also the wife to her husband.
I Corinthians 7:3 NKJV

The Greek word translated as "render" means to "give away" and carries the idea of delivering or giving again. What you render to your spouse is not meant to be a one-time deal. And what you are instructed to render is due benevolence. Let me make it even more plain…give your spouse great sex. How often? As often as it's requested. And since you are a caring spouse, you anticipate their need and offer great sex without their request. It's called "coming on to them." In doing this makes your spouse feel like the king or queen that they are. When you became one through marriage, you signed up to meet each other's needs.

Don't allow time to cause you to stop serving your spouse and start taking them for granted. When you have a servant's mind, you don't allow your feelings to dictate your actions. Where you say, " I don't feel like talking" or "I don't feel like having sex". You do more than you feel. Your spouse is counting on you to meet their needs. If you are truly honest with yourself, you take the feelings out of everything else. Why not sex? Think about this: when you don't feel like going to work, don't you get up and go? When the baby needs to be fed and, it's 3 am and you have to be to work in a few hours. Don't you get up and feed your baby all thou you don't feel like it?

When you don't feel like cooking or even fixing cold cuts, but your kids have to eat. Do you let them starve? No, you pushed your feelings aside, and you fixed the food. Why not do the same when it comes to sex? When I was a firefighter paramedic, I would get 911 calls throughout the day. But after midnight, when I'm showered and in bed, I really want the 911 calls to stop. But they don't. I would have to get up, get dressed, respond, and render care. And I administer great care to people I didn't even know. Although I didn't feel like getting up and going, I took an oath to serve and protect. I had a duty to respond, to serve, and to protect. If I could push my feelings aside for people I didn't even know, why not push my feelings aside for my spouse? And render care, minister love, and have great sex when she is in need. I made a vow to love my spouse (meet her needs) till death do us part. It is imperative that you get your feelings out of the way and have great sex serving your spouse. Doing so will keep satan from getting into your marriage bed.

Lord, help us to lay down our lives today as servants to our spouses.

Do nothing from selfish ambition or conceit, but in humility count others more significant than yourselves. Let each of you look not only to his own interests, but also to the interests of others.
Philippians 2:3-4 ESV

Who's that Peeking in My Window?

Just like marriage is God's idea, having sex is also God's idea. God designed the man and gave him a penis and designed the woman giving her a vagina. The woman was also given a clitoris, which is totally for pleasure. This means that sex is supposed to be a great, pleasurable, and enjoyable time with your spouse. It is God who has given us our sex drive. It is in the written Word of God for Men to be fruitful and multiply and replenish the Earth. How will this take place? By having sex with your spouse. Being sexually intimate with your spouse helps to keep would-be intruders away, as well as bring true happiness and fulfillment to your marriage.

And God blessed them, and God said unto them, Be fruitful, and multiply, and replenish the earth, and subdue it: and have dominion over the fish of the sea, and over the fowl of the air, and over every living thing that moveth upon the earth.
Genesis 1:28 KJV

The devil didn't create sex, nor did he come up with the idea of sex. But he loves to give his input. Satan is a liar and a deceiver. He uses sex to try to control the thermostat of your marriage by controlling the levels of happiness, intimacy, and well-being. He wants to be the thermometer of your marriage and control the overall well-being of the marriage and life, health, stress, conflict, trust, and intimacy of the marriage. Satan is a strategist; he sits and waits for a spouse to open the door and let him in. He's waiting, peeking through the window and watching your bedroom. The question I want to ask is why aren't you watching your bedroom.

Be sober, be vigilant; because your adversary the devil, as a roaring lion, walketh about, seeking whom he may devour
1 Peter 5:8 KJV

Sex is a beautiful gift from God, and He wants us to enjoy it to its fullest. But the enjoyment of sex must be within the protected and committed environment of marriage. Satan doesn't want you to render due benevolence to your spouse. He wants you at odds. He wants you to reject your spouse's need for sex. He wants anger, strife, and conflict to prevail in your marriage. He wants your spouse sexually frustrated so that they go outside of the protected environment of the marriage to find fulfillment. He wants you to be selfish instead of serving and give no thought to the consequences of denying your spouse your sex ministry. Be careful not to bring the baggage of your past loaded with Satan's tricks into your bedroom. Satan's bag of tricks (You're angry, so you won't have sex; you're in your feelings, so you won't have sex; you make excuses so you won't have sex; you play sleep or sick, so you won't have sex, you're thinking of someone else so you won't have sex, you take your spouses need for sex for granted so you won't have sex; you make your spouses need for sex about you so you don't have sex). You must be watchful and vigilant of the marriage bed because sex with your spouse is more than physical.

> *Do not deprive each other [of marital rights], except perhaps by mutual consent for a time, so that you may devote yourselves [unhindered] to prayer, but come together again so that Satan will not tempt you [to sin] because of your lack of self-control.*
> **1 Corinthians 7:5 AMP**

In the above verse of scripture, we see the word deprive, which means don't deny your spouse their marital rights. How would you feel being a law-abiding citizen of a country and you're denied your rights? I'm sure you would not like that at all. Then why would you deny your spouse their marital rights to great sex? Your spouse is supposed to come back to you for more and more. That means you're providing great service, and this is the way God designed it for your spouse to come back to (you) for more sex. Sex is a gift that God gave you for you to give to your spouse.

Sex is More Than Physical, It's Ministry

Why is Stan after your sex life? Why is he watching your bedroom? Satan would rather you masturbate than you have sex with your spouse; this way, he could use your meditation engineering in a vain way, i.e. (Porn or thinking of another person). Satan would prefer you to have sex with someone outside of your marriage covenant than to have sex with your own spouse. He accuses your spouse to you. He intrudes on your thoughts and causes you to think of reasons not to have sex with your spouse. And when you do have sex under Satan's accusatory influence, your demeanor is poor, and your energy is lackluster. Where you lack vitality or conviction, you are uninspired and uninspiring. You see, Satan understands something most married couples don't. He likes it that way; he wants you to remain ignorant and in the blind, this way, he can take advantage of you. He uses an ignorant spouse by causing them to reject their spouse, deny their spouse, or commit infidelity. When apostle Paul recorded the words of God, saying, Render due benevolence. He was literally telling us to render service or ministry to our spouse. Sex is more than physical; it is ministry. Of course, sex is pleasurable and enjoyable, but it is also an undeniable ministry for you and your spouse. Let's see why sex is such a powerful ministry.

That is why a man leaves his father and mother and is united to his wife, and they become one flesh.
Genesis 2:24 NIV

Sex is such a powerful ministry because this is the way God designed a married couple to become one flesh. Sex heals, sex restores, sex refreshes, sex delivers, sex protects, sex bonds two together as one. And Satan knows this, and he doesn't want you operating as one with your spouse. He doesn't want you to have sex with your spouse; he doesn't want you to fulfill your spouse's sexual needs. Satan doesn't want you to bond sexually with your spouse. He doesn't mind you having sex; just don't have it with your spouse.

> *Do you not know that he who unites himself with a prostitute is one with her in body? For it is said, "The two will become one flesh."*
> **1 Corinthians 6:16 NIV**

Let Me Serve You Up

Don't grant the devil access to your spouse through your rejection of their sexual needs, causing them unnecessary temptations, tests, and troubles. Protect your spouse and your marriage through your God-given ministry of sex. Don't give the devil a place; check your demeanor, watch your attitude, make it enjoyable, pleasurable, and pleasing, and render your best sex service. Give your spouse an expectation; tell them, "Let me serve you up; you're the customer." Let them know that sex is on the menu for today, and you can have it your way. Send them a picture, video, or text, and let them know all you can think about is having sex with them. You would be surprised as to the change this would bring into your marriage. You are in control of the thermostat, the levels of happiness and intimacy in your marriage, not Satan. Good sex turns it up; no sex turns it down.

Marriage Satan's Worst Enemy

Satan also knows that he will be defeated by marriage. In the book of Revelation (19:9-21), We see Jesus the husband with the armies of heaven, which is his bride, the church defeat Satan. He is doing all he can to destroy every godly marriage on earth. He attacks the bonding process of becoming one by hindering God's gift of sex. Every time you have sex with your spouse, you defeat Satan. You don't have to feel like you are, but just know that you are. Because you are becoming one in your marriage, paralleling the marriage with Christ. He has prevailed so that you will prevail in your marriage. Have sex, have fun, and enjoy your spouse and marriage. So, how often should you have sex? As often as you like and agree. Remember, each of you may have different sex drives, so push feelings aside and minister to the needs of your spouse. Sex doesn't always have to be the full-course meal. Sometimes you can have quickies, there like having a snack. So, have them often to fill in until dinner is served.

Author bio

Pastors Willie and Sophina Marshall are natives of Tampa and the founders and Senior Leadership of Prevail Christian Church located in the beautiful area of Tampa, FL.

Both having been formally married, they are grateful with having a second chance at marriage and learning to do marriage God's way. Pastor's Willie and Sophina Marshall have a passion to help other married couples experience victory in their marriage.

Willie and Sophina are the host of "The Prevailing Marriage Podcast," a National Podcast heard on several different platforms such as Apple podcast, iHeart radio, Amazon music, and Spotify. Their marriage ministry is real, relevant, and relatable along with their podcast and its purpose is to help Christian couples thrive at having a prevailing marriage. The Marshall's are happily married and have a wonderful, blended family.

Willie & Sophina

God created marriage to be enjoyable, wholesome and bring fulfillment to man and woman. Get the tools you need to have a successful prevailing marriage by listening to the Prevailing Marriage Podcast with pastors Willie and Sophina Marshall.

[theprevailmariagepodcast.com]

FOR MORE INFORMATION
theprevailingmarriage@gmail.com

References:

Mental Toughness for Success
Author: Dr. I.V. Hilliard

The Four Laws of Love
Author: Jimmy Evans

Our Secret Paradise
Author: Jimmy Evans

Marriage on the Rock Certification
Instructor: Jimmy Evans

www.ingramcontent.com/pod-product-compliance
Lightning Source LLC
LaVergne TN
LVHW051502070426
835507LV00022B/2884